Seasonal
Suppers

Seasonal
Suppers

KITCHEN
PRESS

First published in the UK in 2025 by

Kitchen Press Ltd
1 Windsor Place
Dundee DD2 1BG

www.kitchenpress.co.uk

ISBN 9781739174040

A CIP catalogue record for this book is available from
the British Library.

Printed by GPS Group in Bosnia and Herzegovina

This book contains FSC certified paper and other
controlled sources to ensure responsible forest
management.

FSC
MIX
Paper | Supporting
responsible forestry
www.fsc.org
FSC® C118234

8 **January**

18 **February**

28 **March**

38 **April**

50 **May**

60 **June**

70 **July**

80 **August**

92 **September**

102 **October**

114 **November**

126 **December**

136 Delicious Additions
140 Index
144 Acknowledgements

This book is a celebration of the bounty of our seasons, inviting you to embrace the rhythms of nature to create simple, delicious meals from the freshest ingredients. The seasons influence what we choose to eat and even how we eat, from light and elegant dishes in the spring and barbecues in the summer sunshine to the cosy food of autumn and the hearty feasts of winter.

Cooking with seasonal ingredients is a fundamentally practical tradition. It's about being thrifty, making the best of what's good here and now and appreciating the longed-for flavours of new seasons.

The act of sourcing fresh produce from farmers' markets, your own garden or even foraging can be incredibly rewarding and you'll taste the difference. The recipes in this book highlight the best produce available in each season and provide delicious ideas to help you take advantage of what's on offer, whether it be tender asparagus and wild garlic in the spring, juicy, sweet tomatoes in the summer or hearty root vegetables in the colder months.

But convenience is also a factor when deciding what to put on the table, so of the 52 quick and easy dishes in this book, many can be whipped up from basic store-cupboard ingredients – we all know what it feels like having to create something from nothing at dinnertime. I've also included some slightly more elaborate recipes that will be handy for an informal gathering of friends or a simple celebration.

As far as possible, the recipes have been designed to accommodate a 'flexitarian' approach to eating. While they are not all vegetarian, when I can, I've given you options to swap in meat-free alternatives.

Introd

Here are my hot tips for success at suppertime:

Plan. As dull as it sounds, planning takes that last-minute-decision stress off the table. Forewarned is forearmed. Allow enough time to make supper – it's one thing to cook quickly but cooking in a hurry saps energy and takes the joy out of the process.

Substitute depending on what's in season, in your fridge or store cupboard or just according to what you like. For example, spring's Ruffled Filo Asparagus Tart could easily become an autumnal tart with fresh figs, toasted hazelnuts and Brie. Similarly, the Spring Risotto with Asparagus and Lime could easily be made with wild garlic and peas, or with smoked duck and brambles in the autumn. The method stays the same but the season's flavours and fragrances, the things you like, will fit in just as well.

Shop, when you can, in independent food shops: the butcher, the baker, the fishmonger, the fruit and veg shop. The folk that work there are never short of ideas and suggestions if you ask. They know their onions.

V.I.P. yourself. Make your kitchen a place to be happy. Fill it with delicious smells; make it welcoming. Light candles in the dark months, open windows when it's warm and light. Get the tunes on and feel – and know – how important making supper happily is.

I had so much fun with ingredients and ideas in the process of writing this book. I hope it will help you to make the most of what's in season and fill you with inspiration so you can make delicious suppers all year round.

Fi x

A month to couch-dream of mountains to climb this year, then stretch and reflect. We lean on the store cupboard in the dark months, using slow-burning carbs and energising spices, looking for comfort in grains, beans and hearty flavours.

carrot

onion

Janu

Kale

uary

White Bean and Winter Veg Stew

Here is everything you need from a healthy, hearty supper in January. This is my take on a recipe from the wonderful New York Times food section. It's an old-school classic and lemon adds a fresh twist. Serve with focaccia, either shop-bought or homemade (see p.139).

Serves 4

2 tbsp olive oil

1 fennel bulb, finely diced (including frondy tops)

1 medium onion, finely diced

4 large garlic cloves, grated

1 tbsp finely chopped rosemary

¼–½ tsp dried red chilli flakes plus extra to serve

½ tsp fennel seeds

200–250g greens such as kale, rainbow chard or savoy cabbage, washed and finely chopped

2 × 400g tins white beans such as cannellini, haricot or butter beans, drained and rinsed

450ml vegetable stock (I like gel pots)

zest and juice of ½ unwaxed lemon

Parmesan to serve

1 preserved lemon, chopped, to serve

a handful of flat-leaf parsley, chopped, to serve

flaky sea salt and freshly ground black pepper

Heat the olive oil in a large sauté pan or a pan deep enough to take the greens (I use a wok). Add the fennel, onion and garlic and sweat over a low heat for 5 minutes until they soften.

Add the rosemary, chilli flakes and fennel seeds and cook for a minute or so, then add the greens a handful at a time. It will seem like a lot, but the leaves will soon sweat down to a much more manageable size.

Add the beans, increase the heat to medium and cook, stirring, until it sizzles. Add the stock and continue to stir, using the back of your wooden spoon to mash a few beans against the bottom of the pan to thicken and integrate everything. Reduce the heat and simmer for 10 to 12 minutes. If you're in the mood for a big hearty soup, add a bit more stock at this point.

Remove from the heat, add the lemon zest and juice and adjust the seasoning to taste. Serve with a hunk of Parmesan and the grater and little bowls of chopped preserved lemon, chilli flakes and chopped flat-leaf parsley so everyone can customise just as they like.

Stir Fried Rice

You have to work quickly here, so have everything you need ready and on hand. Cook your rice, then rinse it in cold water and store it in a wide dish in the fridge until you need it. This gives the grains a chance to dry and separate and prevents clumps. As a general rule, 200g uncooked rice will yield 600g of cooked rice. This recipe is just as excellent halved for one or two people but don't try to double it – chaos will ensue. Cooking fried rice for a crowd requires *much* bigger pans. Delicious with Chili Crisp (see p.136).

Serves 4

3 tbsp sunflower oil

1 medium onion, finely chopped

4 handfuls (approx. 200–250g) vegetables such as red pepper, courgette, French beans, edamame beans, carrot, petit pois, chopped into small cubes about the size of a corn kernel

200–300g leftover roast chicken or a vegetarian chicken equivalent, chopped into small cubes (optional)

2 tbsp tamari or light soy sauce

1 tbsp mirin

1 tbsp light sesame oil

¼–½ tsp chilli flakes

4 garlic cloves, grated

5cm fresh ginger, peeled and grated

600g cooked jasmine, brown or white long grain rice

2 eggs, lightly whisked, or 100g silken tofu (optional)

1 tbsp rice wine vinegar

25g coriander, chopped

1 lime, cut into wedges

In a wok or high-sided frying pan, heat 1 tablespoon of the sunflower oil over a medium heat, add the onion and fry for 2 to 3 minutes, until it starts to soften and flavour the oil. Add the rest of your veg in stages, starting with the hardest such as carrots, and keep everything moving just enough to prevent it catching and burning. Add the chicken or vegetarian equivalent, if using. Once the veg have become more tender and brighter in colour, after 5 or 6 minutes, transfer everything to a large plate and set aside.

In a small bowl mix the tamari or soy sauce, mirin, sesame oil and chilli flakes together and set aside.

Heat the remaining 2 tablespoons of sunflower oil in the now empty wok or pan and add the garlic and ginger. Stir twice, then add the cooked rice, moving and stirring all the while so it doesn't clump and the garlic and ginger can infiltrate the grains. If using egg or tofu, make a well in the centre of the rice and pour it in, folding the edges of the rice into the centre and repeating a few times. Otherwise, continue to cook, stirring, and after 2 or 3 minutes add the vegetables back in and the tamari mix. Use your spatula to bring everything together, and cook until the rice is hot, fragrant and golden at the edges. Remove from the heat and add the rice wine vinegar and the chopped coriander. Give a final stir and serve in bowls with the lime wedges.

Chicken Cacciatore

Not the quickest dish in the book but it's a delicious crowd pleaser, and once you've chopped the veg the pot can bubble away on the hob. Serve with a green salad and pappardelle drizzled with olive oil and lots of black pepper – or just some nice crusty bread.

Serves 4–6

4 bone-in, skin-on chicken thighs

4 bone-in, skin-on chicken drumsticks

1 tbsp olive oil

25g butter

1 onion, chopped

2 carrots, chopped

2 sticks celery, chopped

3 large garlic cloves, finely chopped

1 tbsp finely chopped rosemary

¼ tsp chilli flakes

200g roasted red peppers from a jar (in oil or brine), drained and chopped

125ml red wine (optional)

1 chicken stock cube or gel pot

2 × 400g tins chopped plum tomatoes

25g basil, chopped

25g flat-leaf parsley, chopped

125g ball of buffalo mozzarella (optional)

flaky salt and freshly ground black pepper

Season the chicken pieces liberally with salt and pepper. In a large deep-sided frying pan or casserole heat the olive oil and butter over a medium heat, then add the chicken. Fry, turning regularly with tongs, until well browned all over, about 8 to 10 minutes. Remove to a large plate to rest.

Pour off all but a tablespoon of oil from your pan and add the onion, carrots and celery. Let them sizzle in the pan juices and soften a little for 3 to 4 minutes, then add the garlic, rosemary, chilli flakes and red peppers, stirring until the oil becomes fragrant, 1 to 2 minutes. Add the wine, if using, and the stock cube, stirring around the base of the pan to dissolve any crispy bits. Add the chicken pieces and the tomatoes and bring to the boil, then reduce the heat to low, give a quick stir, cover and leave to simmer for about 40 minutes until the chicken is tender. Check and correct the seasoning if needed, then scatter with the freshly chopped basil and parsley. If using mozzarella, tear it into pieces and scatter over just before serving.

Soy Mirin Steak Noodles

This dish is everything I aspire to be: rich, intense, refreshing, moreish. Don't be put off by the sugar; it works beautifully to enhance the umami of the soy and the steak.

Serves 4

300–400g sirloin steak at room temperature, patted dry
1 tsp sunflower oil
100ml light soy sauce
50ml mirin
1 tbsp brown sugar
2 garlic cloves, finely chopped
a thumb of fresh ginger, peeled and grated or very finely sliced into julienne
4 spring onions
800ml beef stock, made with best-quality beef stock cubes or gel pots
1 large carrot, peeled into ribbons with a potato peeler
4 nests of dried egg or rice noodles (85g per person)
200g baby spinach leaves
2 tsp toasted sesame seeds
pickled ginger to serve
1 lime, quartered, to garnish
flaky sea salt and freshly ground black pepper

Rub the steak with sunflower oil and season generously on both sides with salt and pepper. Heat a heavy-bottomed frying pan over a medium-high heat until very hot. Lay the steak in the pan, giving it 3 minutes without moving, then turn and repeat on the other side. Whilst the steak is cooking mix together the soy, mirin, brown sugar, garlic and ginger in a shallow bowl big enough to fit the steak. Once the steak is cooked, remove it from the pan and rest it in the soy mixture.

Slice the spring onions into thin strips lengthways, soak in a bowl of ice-cold water and refrigerate until needed.

In a saucepan, bring the beef stock to a simmer, add the carrot ribbons and then the noodles and cook for the time specified on the packet. Meanwhile, thinly slice the rested steak. Pour the soy mixture into the hot beef stock.

To serve, take four bowls and add a handful of baby spinach to each. Divide the carrot and noodles equally between the bowls, then pour over the stock and arrange slices of beef on top. Remove the spring onion curls from the fridge, shake off excess water and scatter over. Finally, sprinkle each bowl with a few sesame seeds and serve with pickled ginger and quarters of lime on the side.

Comfort and simplicity are still needed in the kitchen as we unfurl from the darkest nights. We crave food that fills us up and sustains us. The Earth warms just a little, and emerald green spikes appear like small miracles.

potato

spinach

Febr

cavolo nero

uary

Creamy Cheese Tortellini

This is a super-fast kind of not-macaroni-cheese pasta. You could easily replace the Parmesan with a nice mature Cheddar and it would work a treat. It might seem crazy to add cream cheese but I always have it in my fridge and almost never have actual cream, so this recipe is a bit more 'real' for me. Take care with your timings as tortellini cook in a flash and you can't undo overcooked here.

500g your favourite fresh tortellini (spinach and ricotta work well)
30g butter
3 garlic cloves, grated
¼ tsp chilli flakes
1 tbsp plain flour
300ml whole milk (not skimmed milk)
100g cream cheese
50g Parmesan, freshly grated
10g chives, finely chopped
sea salt and freshly ground black pepper

In a large pot of boiling salted water, cook the tortellini for 2 minutes less than the package instructions and drain well. Set them aside on a plate with a lip so they don't continue to cook and clump together.

Melt the butter in a saucepan over medium heat, add the garlic and chilli flakes and cook, stirring frequently, until fragrant, about 1 minute. Whisk in the flour and cook until lightly browned, about 1 minute. Gradually add the milk, whisking constantly, until slightly thickened, about 2 minutes.

Add the cream cheese and Parmesan and use a wooden spoon to stir into the sauce until melted, about 1 to 2 minutes. If the mixture is too thick, add more milk as needed; taste and season well. Gently fold in the tortellini to combine – you don't want to bash them up. Serve immediately, garnished with chopped chives.

Cacio e Pepe

This is such a rich and indulgent pasta dish and yet it really can be conjured straight from the store cupboard. There's a knack to it but the trick is to prep ahead. Don't start until you have your peppercorns crushed, your cheese finely grated and your jug for saving pasta water beside the stove. Traditionally pecorino is used as it's strong and salty, but we use Parmesan as that's what's always in the fridge.

500g spaghetti or tagliatelle
30g butter
1 tbsp freshly ground/ cracked black pepper
½ tbsp white miso paste
150g Parmesan, pecorino Romano or Grana Padano, or any combination of these, finely grated
15g flat-leaf parsley, finely chopped (optional)

Bring a large pot of well-salted water to a boil, add the pasta and give it a good stir to ensure it doesn't clump. Set a timer for 2 minutes less than the recommended cooking time. While the pasta cooks, melt the butter over a low heat in a large sauté pan and stir in the pepper. Leave to warm over the lowest heat.

When the timer goes off for the pasta, dip a jug into the water and save yourself about 300ml. Set it aside while you drain the pasta.

Add 100ml of the pasta water to the peppery butter in the sauté pan, turn up the heat to medium, stir in the miso, then add the pasta, stirring with a fork rather than a wooden spoon, until every strand is coated. Bring to a simmer (it should only take a minute) and then turn off the heat.

Gradually add the cheese a handful at a time, stirring continuously so it melts and emulsifies into a silky sauce. Add more water if you want more sauce, but do it a little splash and a stir at a time. Don't hang around – serve into warmed bowls and garnish with a handful of chopped flat-leaf parsley, if you're feeling fancy.

Bubble and Squeak

There really are no strict rules for this dish. It's comfort food at its best and possibly the most delicious way to use up leftovers. Spinach, green beans, roasties or boiled new potatoes, parsnips – throw them all in! This is perfect just as it is; however if you have the fixings, poached or fried eggs and bacon is a famously good pairing.

Serves 4

1kg floury potatoes such as Maris Piper or Roosters, peeled and cut into even-sized chunks

3 medium carrots (approx. 400g), cut into 5cm chunks

½ savoy cabbage or 200g kale or cavolo nero, thick stems removed, finely chopped

60g butter, cut into small cubes

100g Cheddar, grated

salt and freshly ground black pepper

In a large saucepan of salted water, bring the potatoes and carrots to the boil and cook until easily pierced with a fork, about 15 minutes. Add the cabbage, kale or cavolo nero for the last 2 minutes of cooking. Preheat the oven to 200°C/180°C fan.

Drain the veg thoroughly and transfer to a large ovenproof frying pan or oven dish. Season well with salt and pepper, sprinkle with the cubes of butter and mash everything together, then scatter over the cheese and put into the oven until the cheese has melted and is bubbling, about 10 minutes. Finish with a final grind of black pepper.

Dijon Honey Chicken Thighs

Truly delicious served with Wonderful Fries (see p.138) – which can go into the oven at the same time as the chicken – and a peppery watercress salad.

Serves 4

8 bone-in, skin-on chicken
  thighs
3 tbsp flour
2 tsp paprika
2 tbsp olive oil
3 tbsp Dijon mustard
2 tbsp wholegrain mustard
2 tbsp runny honey
2 garlic cloves, grated
4–5 sprigs of thyme
salt and freshly ground black
  pepper

Preheat your oven to 200°C/180°C fan. Season the chicken thighs liberally with salt and pepper on both sides. On a large plate mix the flour and paprika and coat the chicken thighs in it. In a small bowl mix 1 tablespoon of the olive oil with the Dijon and wholegrain mustards, honey and garlic and set aside.

In a sauté pan or large ovenproof frying pan, heat the remaining tablespoon of olive oil to medium hot and add the chicken thighs skin-side down. Cook, turning occasionally, until golden brown all over, about 5 to 6 minutes. Turn the thighs so they are skin-side up and drizzle with the honey mustard mix, then tuck the sprigs of thyme in amongst the chicken and put in the oven for 30 to 35 minutes, until cooked. Remove from the oven and allow to rest for 5 minutes before serving.

Light seeps into the days, stretching
them and making mornings a little easier.
Snowdrops and perhaps daffodils on
St David's Day nod in windy March.
Suppers celebrate citrus and spice
and everything nice.

red onion

purple
sprouting
broccoli

Ma

rch

radish

Sri Lankan-Style Dhal

In our highly budget-conscious household, we love dhal. It's quick to prepare and also freezes brilliantly, so I'll often make double the quantity. Serve with rice, flatbreads (see p.138) or – my favourite – a baked sweet potato. If you have time, make the quick sambal; its tangy chilli flavour complements the dhal perfectly.

Serves 4

1 tsp coriander seeds
1 tsp cumin seeds
4 cardamom pods
200g red lentils
2 tbsp olive oil
1 onion, finely chopped
1 green chilli, finely chopped
2 garlic cloves, finely
    chopped
3cm piece of fresh ginger,
    grated
½ tsp turmeric powder
½ tsp cinnamon
1 tbsp garam masala
½ tsp salt
400ml tin coconut milk
15g fresh coriander, roughly
    chopped

for the sambal:
1 fat red chilli, halved,
    deseeded and finely
    chopped
½ red onion, finely chopped
zest and juice of 1 lime
3 tbsp water
1 tbsp olive oil
½ tsp sugar
¼ tsp salt
75g desiccated coconut
    hydrated in 75ml hot water
    for 5 minutes

In a dry frying pan toast the coriander and cumin seeds and cardamom pods until fragrant, then grind them in either a spice grinder or a pestle and mortar (a fairly course consistency is fine). This is an extra step but a quick one and you'll taste the difference.

Wash the lentils in cold water until it runs clear. In a large frying pan heat the olive oil over a medium heat and, when hot, add the finely chopped onion, stirring occasionally until it starts to soften, 2 or 3 minutes. Add the chilli, garlic and ginger, stir it all together and sauté for another 2 minutes. Mix in the ground spice blend and the turmeric, cinnamon, garam masala and salt, and stir well to combine. Then add the lentils, mixing until they are coated with the spices. After about 2 minutes, stir in the coconut milk and 200ml water (just half-fill the empty coconut milk tin). Stir everything and bring to a simmer, then cook, stirring occasionally, for 20 minutes.

Meanwhile, mix all the sambal ingredients together in a bowl. Sprinkle the dhal with the chopped coriander and serve with sambal on the side.

Tempura Everything

It's a bit of a treat to have tempura and surprisingly versatile as you can really get creative with what you batter. Prep ahead as you want to be going straight from the wok to the plate with no hanging around. Make sure each item is dry before dipping in the batter as otherwise the batter won't stick.

Serves 4

for the dipping sauce:
3 tbsp soy sauce
2 tbsp rice wine vinegar
1 tbsp runny honey
1 tbsp finely chopped fresh
   ginger

125g plain flour
125g cornflour
1 tsp sea salt
1 egg yolk
250ml ice-cold sparkling
   water
400g (approx.) mix of veg
   such as red, green or
   yellow pepper, sweet
   potato, courgette,
   asparagus, broccoli, sugar
   snap peas, mushrooms,
   radishes, sprigs of fresh
   basil, curly kale, dried well
   and thinly sliced or cut into
   bite-sized pieces
8–12 king prawns, shelled
   and deveined
sunflower oil for frying

Mix all the dipping sauce ingredients together, divide between four little bowls and place next to your supper plates on the table. Make the batter by whisking the flour, cornflour and salt together in a large bowl. In a separate bowl, lightly beat the egg yolk with a fork, then mix it with the ice-cold sparkling water. Gradually add the wet ingredients into the flour while mixing lightly and quickly with the fork until just combined – don't worry about the odd lump.

Heat 3 to 4cm of sunflower oil in your wok. The oil is hot enough when a drop of the tempura batter sizzles and quickly rises to the surface when you drop it in. Line a baking tray with kitchen paper to absorb excess oil and place next to the cooker. Using either tongs or chopsticks, dip each item into the batter, gently shake off any excess, then carefully place it into the hot oil. Fry only a few pieces at a time to avoid overcrowding. Fry until the tempura is very lightly golden and crispy, about 2 to 3 minutes per batch. Use a slotted spoon to transfer the cooked tempura to your prepared baking tray. Serve the tempura immediately, while hot and crispy. Dip in the sauce and enjoy.

Herby Rice and Citrus Prawns

This is a pretty easy one-pot cracker. The marinade for the prawns is almost a ceviche marinade on purpose – we want the prawns to tenderise and cook in the citrus before they're steamed in with the rice. Serve with a big well-dressed salad and lots of warm bread to soak up the delicious juices.

for the marinade:
juice of 1 lemon
juice of 1 lime
juice of 1 orange
1 small red onion, finely
  sliced
1 green chilli, finely chopped
1 bay leaf

500g king prawns, shelled
  and deveined
1 green pepper, roughly
  chopped
1 small white onion, roughly
  chopped
a thumb of fresh ginger,
  peeled and roughly
  chopped
2 garlic cloves, peeled
30g coriander
30g flat-leaf parsley
1 tsp fine sea salt
600ml vegetable stock
60ml extra virgin olive oil
300g jasmine rice, or other
  long grain rice, rinsed well

First make the marinade: in a large bowl, mix the lemon, lime and orange juices, onion, chilli and bay leaf. Add the prawns to the bowl, mix so they are well coated and set aside somewhere cool to marinate.

Add the green pepper, white onion, ginger, garlic, coriander, parsley and salt to a blender or food processor. Pour in half the stock and blitz until puréed, then add the other half of the stock and give a few pulses to combine.

In a large saucepan or sauté pan with a lid, heat the olive oil over a medium heat, add the rice and stir, allowing it to toast for 2 to 3 minutes. Add the herby stock to the rice, allow it to come to a boil, then turn the heat to very low and simmer, covered, for 10 to 12 minutes. Now quickly mix the marinated prawns and their marinade into the rice, put the lid straight back on and give it another 3 minutes. Take the rice off the heat and leave the pan to sit with the lid on for another 10 minutes before serving.

Toad in the Hole with Red Onion Gravy

Part magic trick, part comfort food classic. After years of making this I still get a thrill seeing the towering edges of Yorkshire when you open the oven door. Serve with green beans, mash and this stellar red onion gravy. Vegetarians, simply substitute veggie sausages and stock.

Serves 4

2 tbsp sunflower oil (3 tbsp if using veggie sausages)
6–8 sausages (regular or veggie ones)
150g plain flour
4 medium eggs
½ tsp salt
250ml whole milk (not skimmed milk)

for the red onion gravy:
1 tbsp oil
15g butter
2 red onions, thinly sliced
2 tsp runny honey or sugar
1 tsp plain flour
500ml beef or veggie stock
1 tbsp wholegrain mustard (optional)
1 small sprig of thyme or rosemary, leaves finely chopped
fine sea salt and freshly ground black pepper

Preheat the oven to 240°C/220°C fan. Add the oil and then the sausages to a large metal roasting dish with high sides. Give the dish a shake to coat the sausages in the oil, then put into the oven for 10 minutes or until the sausages are golden. Meanwhile, in a large bowl whisk the flour into the eggs until it is very smooth. Add the salt and half the milk, whisk again until smooth, then add the rest of the milk and whisk again.

When your sausages are golden, remove them from the oven, pour the batter all around them and put the dish straight back in the oven. Now, turn the temperature down to 200°C/180°C fan, set the timer for 30 minutes and resist – resist! – the temptation to look in at your toads until the timer goes off.

Make the gravy. Over a medium heat, melt the oil and butter in a frying pan. Add the onions and honey or sugar, and season. Turn down the heat and cook for about 15 minutes, stirring occasionally, until the onions are tender and slightly caramelised. Sprinkle over the flour and stir, then turn up the heat to medium and allow the flour to soak up the juices and brown a little. Then slowly add the hot stock, stirring continuously, so it continues to simmer, and stir in the mustard, if using, and the finely chopped thyme or rosemary.

Remove the toad in the hole from the oven and serve with a jug of gravy so everyone can help themselves.

Lambs, blossom, blue skies and puffy white clouds, new shoots and wild garlic. Spring emerges into the world like opening the pages of a pop-up book. We savour later sunsets, hearty, filling broths and the fresh, warming heat of chilli and spices.

spring onion

spring greens

ril

garlic

Wild Garlic Gnudi with Brown Butter and Lemon

This is how you can enjoy light clouds of cheese with a nutty, buttery sauce in a matter of minutes. If you don't have wild garlic, use fresh basil or spinach. Serve with crusty bread and a pea shoot salad.

Serves 4

150g wild garlic leaves, washed
500g ricotta, excess whey drained
100g panko
2 medium egg yolks
zest of 1 lemon
½ tsp fine sea salt
½ tsp fresh ground black pepper

for the sauce:
100g fresh or frozen garden peas
60g salted butter
juice of the zested lemon
25g basil, finely chopped at the last minute (optional)
50g Parmesan, finely grated (optional)

Blanch the wild garlic in boiling salted water for 30 seconds, then plunge into ice-cold water to stop the cooking process. When the leaves are cool, drain them and squeeze out as much of the water as you can. Pat the leaves dry and finely chop them. Chopping will take 2 minutes to be thorough; you don't want any large straggly pieces as these will cause your gnudi to fall apart.

Line a sieve with a two sheets of kitchen paper and put the ricotta in, flattening it out with the back of a spoon. If you don't have a big enough sieve, lay the kitchen paper on a plate and do the same. Cover with another two sheets and gently press a bit more. Leave to drain for 10 minutes while you get everything else together.

Put the wild garlic, panko, egg yolks, lemon zest, seasoning and the patted ricotta (peeled off the kitchen paper) in a large bowl. Mix well using a spatula, then use your hands to form into little balls roughly the diameter of a 50p piece. Lightly blanch the peas by pouring boiling water over them in a bowl and setting aside.

Over a medium-low heat, in a large non-stick frying pan, add the butter and allow to melt and slowly turn brown, which should take 1 or 2 minutes but don't hurry the process. Once the butter is golden brown, add the little gnudi dumplings. Turn up the heat a fraction and cook for 1 to 2 minutes, shaking the pan from time to time to keep them turning in the butter. Now add the juice from the zested lemon and allow it to sizzle a bit. Drain the peas and add them to the pan with the gnudi, gently shaking rather than stirring to keep the gnudi intact. Season with a pinch each of sea salt and freshly ground black pepper and scatter with the chopped fresh basil and Parmesan, if using.

Ruffled Filo Asparagus Tart

Pretty effortless, completely delicious and it looks impressive too. Serve warm, preferably with lightly dressed baby leaves, radishes and a new potato salad.

Serves 4

100g crème fraîche
1 egg
1 tsp finely chopped
  rosemary
1 garlic clove, grated
zest of 1 lemon
150g Boursin or Le Roulé
  garlic and herb soft cheese
75g butter, melted
½ tsp fine sea salt
12 sheets filo pastry
100g asparagus tips
30g Parmesan, finely grated
15g chives, flat-leaf parsley
  or tarragon, finely chopped
freshly ground black pepper

33 × 23cm rimmed baking
  tray

Preheat your oven to 200°C/180°C fan. Make the tart filling by whisking together the crème fraîche, egg, rosemary, garlic, half the lemon zest and the Boursin or Le Roulé until it is the thickness of double cream then set aside.

Melt the butter in a small pan and stir in the sea salt. Lightly dampen a clean tea towel. Open the filo sheets and store under the damp tea towel while you work. Take one sheet and, using a pastry brush, paint with the salty butter and lay another sheet on top. Now use both hands to ruffle the double sheet, like fabric, so it wrinkles and folds, and place it in the baking tray. Repeat another 5 times so the baking tray is filled with ruffled sheets of filo, with some loose parts and some more dense ruffles. Brush the tops of the ruffles with any leftover melted butter.

Lay the asparagus amongst the ruffles, some sticking out, some hidden. Gently pour the filling mixture over the pastry, making sure it's evenly distributed. Scatter over the grated Parmesan and place the tart in the oven for 20 to 24 minutes, until the filling is set and the filo is golden. Remove from the oven and allow to cool for 10 minutes before transferring from the baking tray onto a cooling rack to prevent the bottom from going soggy. Top with the remaining lemon zest, chopped chives and a few grinds of black pepper and eat while still warm.

Vietnamese Rice Paper Rolls

The process of assembling these is straightforward once you get a handle on it, and it can be great fun to set up all the components at the table and let people roll their own. You could add other vegetables such as cucumber or radishes as well as or instead of the red pepper, and vegetarians can substitute tofu for the prawns.

Serves 4

1 large carrot
zest and juice of 1 lime
1 tsp sugar
1 tsp salt
150g vermicelli rice noodles
12 sheets (or more) of
  rice paper about 20cm
  diameter
200g cooked king prawns,
  cut in half from top to
  bottom
1 red pepper, deseeded and
  cut into thin strips
30g mint, stems discarded
15g basil, thick stems
  discarded
30g coriander

for the dipping sauce:
100ml hoisin sauce
60g peanut butter
  (smooth or chunky)
1 garlic clove, grated or finely
  chopped
15ml rice vinegar (or white
  wine vinegar will do)

Finely cut the carrot into thin strands. Put it in a bowl and sprinkle over the lime juice and zest, the sugar and the salt and mix well with your fingertips. Allow to marinate for 10 minutes or so whilst you prepare everything else.

Cook the vermicelli rice noodles according to the packet instructions and rinse well in cold water as soon as they're cooked. Snip them a couple of times with scissors when they are cool in the bowl to make it easier to get a portion size. Prepare the rest of your ingredients and place in bowls within easy reach. Have a wide shallow bowl with warm water ready for the rice paper sheets.

To make a roll, dip your rice paper into the warm water for a couple of seconds at most – completely submerge it, then quickly take it out and lay it on a clean plate or board. Work within an imaginary centre rectangle and lay your first ingredients down so the most attractive side is facing the rice paper. I normally do three halves of prawn, then some carrot, vermicelli, pepper slices, a few leaves each of mint and basil and a decent sprig of coriander. Then fold the rice paper edge closest to you up and over the ingredients, bring in the sides and roll it over until it's sealed.

Make a dipping sauce by whisking the hoisin, peanut butter, garlic and rice vinegar in a medium bowl. Add water a tablespoon at a time until it's the consistency of double cream and serve alongside the rolls.

Delicious Vegan Laksa

Any kind of noodle is good in this aromatic and spicy coconut soup. And it's easy to find laksa paste that doesn't contain shrimp, so that's the direction I've taken here. Of course, you could change out the tofu for chicken, prawns or cubes of white fish.

Serves 4

200g rice vermicelli noodles
1 tbsp vegetable oil
1 bunch spring onions, trimmed and finely chopped
200g firm tofu, cut into 1cm cubes
2 tbsp laksa paste
400ml coconut milk
500ml vegetable stock
150g asparagus, woody ends snapped off
100g spring greens, washed and finely chopped
1 red chilli, deseeded and thinly sliced
30g coriander, chopped, to garnish
1 lime, cut into wedges

Prepare the rice vermicelli noodles according to the package instructions. Drain and set aside. In a large saucepan, heat the vegetable oil over medium heat, add the spring onion and sauté for 2 to 3 minutes until softened. Add the tofu, then stir in the laksa paste and cook for 2 to 3 minutes, until everything is coated and starting to cook.

Pour in the coconut milk and vegetable stock and bring the mixture to a gentle simmer. Prepare the asparagus by slicing into ribbons using a vegetable peeler along the length of the spears and add to the simmering broth with the finely chopped spring greens.

Divide the cooked rice vermicelli noodles among your serving bowls, and ladle the hot laksa broth over the noodles, making sure to distribute the tofu and green beans evenly. Top each bowl with a few slices of red chilli, some chopped coriander and a lime wedge for squeezing over the laksa before enjoying.

Turkey Meatballs with Tahini Sauce

Serve with a big green salad. Chicken can be substituted for the turkey with equally delicious results.

Serves 4

2 medium red onions, sliced into thick crescents

2 medium sweet potatoes, cut into 3cm chunks

2 red/yellow/orange peppers (any combination), deseeded and cut into 3cm chunks

5 tbsp olive oil

1 medium egg

70g panko

1 medium courgette, grated

zest of 1 lime

1 tsp ground cumin

1 tsp ground coriander

2 garlic cloves, grated

1 plump red serrano chilli, deseeded and finely chopped

500g turkey mince

fine sea salt and freshly ground black pepper

for the tahini sauce:

1 garlic clove, grated

3 tbsp light tahini, well mixed

3 tbsp water

juice of the zested lime

¼ tsp sea salt

1 tsp maple syrup or honey

Preheat the oven to 220°C/200°C fan. Line a large, rimmed roasting tray with greaseproof and add the red onion, sweet potato and peppers. Drizzle over 3 tablespoons of the olive oil, season well, then roast in the oven for 15 minutes.

In a medium-sized mixing bowl, lightly whisk the egg and stir in the panko. Squeeze as much water as you can from the grated courgette with your hands and add to the bowl with the lime zest, ground cumin and coriander, garlic, chilli and a teaspoon of sea salt. Add the turkey mince and, using clean hands, incorporate everything really well, then divide and roll the mixture into 12 to 16 roughly golf-ball-sized meatballs.

When the vegetables have had 15 minutes in the oven, take them out and use a spatula to turn them, then add the turkey meatballs, nestling them into the veg. Drizzle with the remaining 2 tablespoons of olive oil, then return to the oven for another 20 minutes, turning after 10 minutes so they cook through. When done the meatballs should be brown all over with no hint of pink when you break one in half.

Whisk up all the tahini sauce ingredients, drizzle the sauce over the vegetables and meatballs and serve.

Beltane and hawthorn, forget-me-nots and comets, birdsong and the dawn chorus. Where does the time go? Nearly half the year gone! Suppers can be quick and irresistible, with dishes that can easily be eaten in the garden if the chance arises.

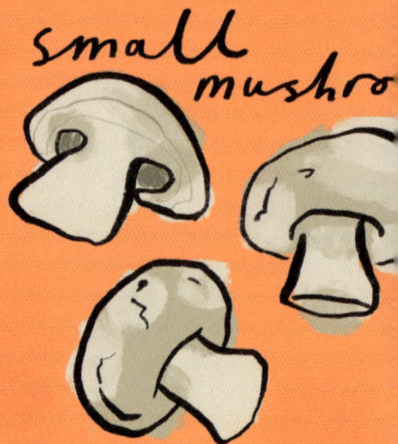

small mushro

asparagus

coriander

peas

ay

Spring Risotto with Asparagus and Lime

Use any spring salad leaves you can get your hands on. For simplicity, the risotto is prepared in the same pan you fry your asparagus in.

Serves 4

3 tbsp olive oil

250g asparagus, woody ends snapped off

zest of 1 lime, a pinch reserved

250g onions or shallots, finely chopped

250g Arborio rice

250ml dry white wine

900ml vegetable stock, hot

50g butter, cubed

30g Parmesan, freshly grated, plus extra to serve

100g salad leaves such as rocket, wild garlic, pea shoots, fennel tips, radish leaves

fine sea salt and freshly ground black pepper

Heat 1 tablespoon of olive oil in a large heavy-based sauté pan. Add the asparagus and fry over a high heat until it begins to sear in places, about 2 minutes. Tip onto a plate, cut into 5cm pieces, season, scatter with lime zest (reserving a pinch for later) and set aside.

Add the rest of the olive oil to the pan, then the onions or shallots and cook over a low heat until soft and starting to turn golden, about 6 to 7 minutes. Turn up the heat, add the rice and stir so each grain is coated in oil. After a minute, when the rice has started to turn translucent, add the white wine to the pan and stir until it has been absorbed.

Turn the heat down a bit, add a third of the stock and keep stirring until it's almost completely absorbed. Add the rest of the stock 300ml at a time until it's all been absorbed and the rice has started to become tender and creamy, about 18 minutes. Each grain of rice should still be individual.

Stir in the butter a couple of pieces at a time and fold in the asparagus and grated Parmesan. Season and add a last pinch of lime zest. Top with a good grating or shavings of Parmesan and a handful of leaves and serve.

Mushroom Risotto variation
Substitute the same quantity of sliced mushrooms for the asparagus, and fry them in two batches until golden. Use lemon instead of lime.

Quick and Easy Falafels

You can go to town on the accompaniments by adding pitta or flatbreads (see p.138), Tahini Dressing (see p.136) and Zhoug (see p.137), but if you're pressed for time just make the speedy lemon mayo (see below).

Serves 4–6

1 × 400g tin chickpeas, drained and rinsed
15g flat-leaf parsley or coriander, roughly chopped
½ medium onion, roughly chopped
2 garlic cloves, crushed
1 tsp ground coriander
1 tsp ground cumin
1 tbsp fresh lemon juice
4 tbsp (35g) flour
1 tsp baking powder
fine sea salt and freshly ground black pepper

sunflower oil for frying

for the lemon mayo:
4 tbsp mayo (I like Hellmann's)
1 tbsp freshly squeezed lemon juice
freshly ground black pepper

Combine the chickpeas, parsley or coriander, onion, garlic, ground coriander and cumin, lemon juice, a ½ teaspoon of salt and plenty of black pepper in the bowl of a food processor and pulse until it all starts to come together. Add the flour and baking powder and pulse again until incorporated. The mixture should be dry enough to handle and mould – if it's too wet, add another tablespoon of flour, and if it's too dry, a splash of water or a squeeze of lemon juice should fix it.

Using two spoons, one to scoop up the mix and one to scrape off, form rough patties. They needn't be too perfect, but it's helpful if they're a uniform size. A slightly flattened shape cooks more evenly than balls.

Heat 1cm sunflower oil in a frying pan over a medium heat and fry in batches until the falafels are golden and crisp, about 2 to 3 minutes on each side. Once cooked place on a kitchen-paper-lined plate.

Mix the mayo with the lemon juice and several grinds of black pepper and serve with the falafels and your choice of accompaniments.

Trout with Herb and Lime Crust

This is the Nigel Slater recipe that changed everything for me – the first thing I chose to cook from *Real Fast Food,* the greatest cookery book ever written. Serve with steamed peas and some buttery new potatoes for the perfect quick supper.

Serves 4

2 slices stale wholemeal
   bread, crusts cut off, or
   50g panko
zest of 2 limes
10g basil, finely chopped
10g flat-leaf parsley, finely
   chopped
2 tbsp olive oil
4 × 140g (approx.) trout
   fillets, trimmed and
   checked for bones
juice of 1 lime
1 lime, quartered, to serve
sea salt and freshly ground
   black pepper

Preheat the oven to 200°C/180°C fan. If you're making your own breadcrumbs, tear the bread into the bowl of a food processor, add the lime zest and a pinch of sea salt and blitz until you have fine crumbs. Add the finely chopped basil and parsley and pulse briefly to combine. If using panko, simply add the lime zest, salt and herbs to a bowl and mix together.

Line a rimmed baking tray with greaseproof paper, drizzle over a tablespoon of the olive oil and sprinkle with a little salt, then lay the trout fillets on the paper. Season the top of each fillet with salt and freshly ground black pepper, then squeeze the lime juice over and heap a quarter of the breadcrumbs on each fillet, pressing firmly so the crumbs stick to the fish. Drizzle the remaining tablespoon of olive oil over the top and put in the oven. Bake until the trout is cooked through and the crumbs are golden, about 10 to 12 minutes. Serve with the quarters of lime.

Rigatoni Marinara with Bacon and Rosemary Breadcrumbs

It might seem odd adding bacon breadcrumbs here, but they bring great texture and a lovely smoky flavour. You may have leftover breadcrumbs, but they'll keep for ages in the fridge and are a magical addition to dhal or a bowl of soup.

May

for the bacon and rosemary
breadcrumbs:

3 tbsp extra virgin olive oil

2 strips smoked streaky
bacon, or vegetarian alt,
finely chopped

1 large garlic clove, grated

1 tsp finely chopped
rosemary

75g panko

3 tbsp extra virgin olive oil

2 garlic cloves, peeled and
crushed

1 tsp fennel seeds

¼–½ tsp chilli flakes

2 × 400g tins chopped
tomatoes

2 tsp runny honey

1–2 tsp red wine vinegar

500g pasta such as rigatoni
or penne

25g cold butter, cut into
small cubes

1 tbsp finely chopped
rosemary

fine sea salt and freshly
ground black pepper

In a large saucepan with a lid, heat the olive oil over a medium heat for a minute, then add the bacon and fry until it starts to brown and crisp. Turn down the heat a little and add the garlic, mixing well before adding the rosemary, panko and a big pinch of sea salt. Stir until the panko is golden and fragrant, then transfer to a clean plate and set aside.

In the same pan, over a low-to-medium heat, add the olive oil, then the crushed garlic, fennel seeds and chilli flakes. Allow to bloom and become fragrant in the oil for 2 to 3 minutes (taking care not to allow the garlic to burn), then add the tomatoes, honey, vinegar and a pinch of salt and stir well. Bring to the boil, then turn down and leave to simmer for 15 to 20 minutes while you cook the pasta.

Cook your pasta in well-salted boiling water according to the packet instructions. Drain swiftly, reserving a small amount of water (roughly 50ml). Add the pasta to the sauce along with just enough reserved water to give the sauce some gloss. Finish by stirring in the butter and rosemary, then serve with a generous scattering of the garlicky, bacon breadcrumbs over the top.

Here are the longest and lightest days.
Limbs stretched on dry grass at last for
midsummer parties and picnics with
tacos, tortillas and fragrant salads.
Early morning sunshine and light into
the night make this the easy picky,
park-y supper season.

garlic

cucumber

Ju

lettuce

Cheddar and Parsley Spanish Tortilla

Keep it simple or top your tortilla with tender salad leaves and sliced vine tomatoes. Best eaten warm but wonderful eaten cold too (especially on a picnic!), and it will keep for up to 3 days in the fridge.

Serves 4

100ml olive oil for frying

3–4 medium potatoes (approx. 500g), peeled and sliced as thinly as possible

2 medium onions, finely sliced

2 garlic cloves, chopped

a handful of flat-leaf parsley, chopped

6 large eggs

125g grated cheese (I like Isle of Mull Cheddar)

flaky sea salt and freshly ground black pepper

In a medium non-stick frying pan that's at least 4cm deep, heat the oil on medium-high. Season the potato slices with plenty of salt and pepper.

When the oil is very hot (a potato slice sizzles when dropped in), gently slip the potatoes into the oil. Fry for about 5 minutes, turning occasionally (trying not to break them) and adjusting the heat so they sizzle but don't brown. Then add the onions and garlic and continue to cook for another 6 or 7 minutes, until the potatoes are soft and the onions are translucent. Remove from the pan onto a plate lined with kitchen paper or a colander set over a bowl to catch some of the excess oil. Reserve 1 tablespoon of the oniony oil. Add the chopped parsley to the potato-onion mixture.

Crack the eggs into a large bowl, season and beat with a fork. Add the potato-onion mixture and the cheese to the eggs and stir gently to combine, trying not to break the potatoes (some will anyway).

Heat the pan on medium-high. Add the tablespoon of reserved oil. Let the oil get very hot (so the eggs don't stick), then pour in the potato and egg mixture, spreading it evenly. Cook for a minute, then lower the heat to medium-low, cooking until the tortilla is set at the edges, halfway set in the centre and it easily slips around in the pan when you give it a shake, 8 to 10 minutes.

Set a flat, rimless plate that's at least as wide as the pan upside down over the pan. Lift the skillet off the burner and, with one hand against the plate, invert the skillet so the tortilla lands on the plate. Set the pan back on the heat and slide the tortilla into it. Tuck in the edges and cook over a low heat until a skewer inserted into the centre comes out clean, another 5 to 7 minutes. Transfer the tortilla to a serving platter and let cool at least 10 minutes before eating.

Spaghetti Aglio e Olio

Also known as 'midnight pasta' in my house, this simple, delicious store-cupboard dish takes 15 minutes from beginning to end. Beloved of chefs, late-night revelers and burners of the midnight oil. Melt a couple of anchovy fillets in with the garlic for an extra flavour kick.

Serves 4

500g spaghetti, bucatini or linguine
75ml (a good glug) extra virgin olive oil
8–10 garlic cloves, crushed
½ tsp chilli flakes
zest and juice of ½ lemon (optional)
25g flat-leaf parsley or basil, tough stems removed, leaves chopped
Parmesan to serve
fine sea salt and freshly ground black pepper

Bring a large pan of well-salted water to the boil and cook the pasta for 2 minutes less than the packet instructions. Meanwhile, heat the olive oil in a large frying or sauté pan over a medium heat and add the garlic. Keep an eye on it, stirring occasionally, until it starts to become fragrant and turns a light golden brown, about 6 to 7 minutes. Add the chilli flakes and swirl, then turn the heat down very low while you drain the pasta.

Just before draining the pasta, dip a mug or jug in to reserve some cooking water. Then drain and add the pasta to the sauté pan along with about 100ml (half a mug) of the reserved pasta water. Turn up the heat to medium and, using tongs, toss the spaghetti until it's completely dressed in the garlicky olive oil.

Add the lemon zest and juice, if using, lots of freshly ground black pepper, salt if you need it and the chopped parsley or basil. Divide between bowls and serve with a good hunk of Parmesan and the grater so people can help themselves.

Roasted Salmon Tacos with Avocado Crema

Super easy, quick to throw together and always a hit with the kids.
Feel free to use whatever veg you have on hand instead of or as well
as the red pepper – sugar snap peas and radishes both work well.

for the spice mix:
1 tbsp soft brown sugar
1½ tsp fine sea salt
1½ tsp sweet paprika
1½ tsp garlic powder
1 tsp freshly ground black
  pepper

500–600g Scottish
  salmon fillet, trimmed
  and pinboned or 4 × 110g
  pieces of salmon
1 tbsp extra virgin olive oil

for the avocado crema:
1 ripe avocado
1 garlic clove, grated
150g crème fraîche or
  soured cream
juice of 1 lime
15g coriander, roughly
  chopped

12 small tortillas
½ iceberg lettuce, finely
  chopped
1 red pepper, deseeded and
  sliced into strips

Preheat the oven to 190°C/170°C fan. In a small bowl, combine the sugar, salt, sweet paprika, garlic powder and pepper. Line a baking tray with a double layer of greaseproof paper and lay the salmon on it, skin-side down. Brush the salmon with the olive oil, then rub the spice mix over until the exposed side is completely covered. Bake until the salmon is cooked through and flakes easily with a fork, approximately 18 to 20 minutes for a 600g fillet and 12 to 15 minutes for 110g pieces. Check your salmon at the minimum cooking time as it will continue to cook for a couple of minutes after you've taken it out of the oven.

Meanwhile, make the avocado crema by mashing the avocado, garlic, crème fraîche or soured cream, lime juice and coriander in a medium bowl. Warm the tortillas in a hot, dry frying pan, 30 seconds per side, and keep warm. Serve with the chopped lettuce and pepper on the table so everyone can assemble their tacos themselves.

Roasted Cauliflower Tacos variation
Substitute a large cauliflower for the salmon. Preheat your oven to 200°C/180°fan. Cut the cauliflower into florets and toss in 2 tablespoons of olive oil in a large bowl, then add the spice mix and toss until the florets are fully coated. Roast for 30 minutes on a baking tray lined with greaseproof paper.

Sticky Lemongrass Chicken Salad

The chicken can be prepared and left to marinate in the fridge overnight. That said, it will be just as delicious if you leave it on the countertop for 20 minutes while you prepare the rest of the salad. I like to serve this with a steaming mountain of rice or sesame noodles.

June

Serves 4

2 stalks lemongrass, tender
  inner part finely chopped
4 garlic cloves, grated
a thumb of ginger, peeled
  and grated
1 tbsp fish sauce
zest and juice of 1 lime
2 tbsp honey
2 tbsp soy sauce
2 tbsp vegetable oil
1 tsp fine sea salt
8–10 boneless, skinless
  chicken thighs

for the salad:
2 medium cucumbers
2 tbsp runny honey
juice of 1 lime
1 tbsp fish sauce
1 tbsp rice vinegar
1 butterhead lettuce, leaves
  separated and washed
2 tbsp chopped roasted
  peanuts
2–3 spring onions, sliced
  thinly on the diagonal
10g coriander leaves to
  garnish
10g mint leaves to garnish
10g chives to garnish

Preheat your oven to 200°C/180°C fan. Add the lemongrass, garlic, ginger, fish sauce, lime zest and juice, honey, soy, vegetable oil and salt to a large bowl. Trim any excess fat from the chicken and discard. Add the thighs to the bowl and toss in the marinade so they are completely coated. Wrap the bowl and refrigerate for up to 24 hours, or just leave to marinate on the countertop while you get on with the salad.

Peel and halve the cucumbers, then cut into largish diagonal pieces. In a bowl, whisk together the honey, lime juice, fish sauce and vinegar, then mix in the cucumber and set aside.

Line a rimmed baking tray with greaseproof paper. Remove the chicken from the marinade, place on the prepared baking tray and bake for 25 to 30 minutes, basting once or twice while it's cooking. Test it's done by pressing the fattest chicken thigh with a fork to see if the juices run clear. When the chicken is ready, remove it from the oven to rest while you arrange the lettuce on a serving plate and scatter over the cucumber and its dressing. Transfer the chicken pieces to the plate and finish with a sprinkling of the chopped peanuts, spring onions and fresh herbs.

There's a gentle, easy-going hum on the streets as people sit out and warm their bones. Light late into the night and the air in the city is full of the smell of hot olive oil and garlic from restaurants and park barbecues. Delicious suppers and hot pavements sizzle to summer playlists and a cold glass of something quenching.

nectarine

courgette

beetroot

Neon Pasta

This technicolour pasta looks the part and it follows through on taste too, with the warm earthy beetroot uplifted by the lime, chilli and ginger. If you're having a barbecue, this goes perfectly with anything hot off the grill. You can buy cooked, unvinaigered beetroot in the supermarket if you don't have time to boil your own.

Serves 4

4 fresh beetroot or
  shop-bought cooked,
  unvinaigered beetroot
2 tbsp extra virgin olive oil
100g light tahini
2 tbsp tamari or soy sauce
a thumb of fresh ginger,
  peeled and grated
1 large garlic clove, peeled
  and grated
zest and juice of 1 lime

350g linguini or spaghetti
1 sweet potato (approx.
  200g), scrubbed and dried
1 red serrano chilli, deseeded
  and finely chopped
100g feta, roughly crumbled
50g unsalted pistachios,
  roughly chopped
20g basil, thick stems
  removed
1 tsp sesame oil
1 tsp flaky sea salt

If using fresh beetroot, boil them in their skins in salted water until easily pierced with a knife, then peel them when cool enough to handle. Make a sauce by blitzing the beetroot with the olive oil, tahini, tamari or soy, ginger, garlic and lime zest and juice in a food processor or with a stick blender.

Cook the linguini or spaghetti in salted boiling water according to the instructions on the packet. While the pasta is cooking, peel the sweet potato, cut into thin slices and then cut the slices into matchstick-width strands. Put the sweet potato into the pasta water for the last 30 seconds of cooking, then drain with the pasta and rinse both in cold water. You don't want to cook the sweet potato fully or it will fall apart; you just want to tenderise it a little bit.

In a large bowl (or the now-cool pasta pan), mix the pasta and sweet potato with the beetroot sauce and transfer to your serving dish. Scatter over the finely chopped red chilli, the crumbled feta, the chopped pistachios and the basil. Finally, drizzle with the sesame oil, sprinkle with the salt and serve.

Sea Bass with Lime Courgettes and Ginger

This is as delicious cold as it is hot. Serve it with a big green salad with coriander and finely sliced red chilli and some new potatoes. The fish is cooked in a parcel and you can make a great dressing by mixing the juices that collect in it with a little tamari and a pinch of sugar. Rainbow trout, sole, plaice or halibut would also be lovely here.

Serves 4

2 medium courgettes, topped and tailed

zest and juice of 2 limes

2 tbsp extra virgin olive oil

1 tbsp coriander seeds, toasted (optional)

4 × 180–200g sea bass fillets

4–6 spring onions, sliced into fine strips

a thumb of fresh ginger, peeled and very finely sliced into thin strands

100ml rosé or white wine

50ml sunflower oil

50ml sesame oil

flaky sea salt and freshly ground black pepper

Preheat the oven to 220°C/200°C fan. Either slice the courgettes into thin strips or use a vegetable peeler to slice them into thin ribbons, stopping when you hit the softer centre, and rotating to repeat. Discard the two soft cores. Put the courgette strips in a large bowl and add the lime zest and juice, the olive oil, a pinch of salt and the toasted coriander seeds, if using.

Place a large piece of baking parchment on a baking tray with raised edges. Position the paper so you'll be able to fold it into a parcel. Place the courgette in the centre of the parchment and arrange to make a bed for the fish. Pat the fish dry, season it, then lay it on top of the courgette. Scatter the spring onions and the finely sliced ginger over the fish.

Fold up the sides of the parchment so the base won't leak and pour in the wine. Then fold the edges of the paper together and crimp the edges to seal the parcel. Put it in the oven and bake until the fish is just cooked through, about 12 to 15 minutes, depending on the thickness of the fish.

Heat the oils in a small pan over a medium heat until hot. When the fish is ready, open up the parcel, drizzle over the hot oil and let it sizzle and mix with the lime and olive oil from the courgette. Irresistible!

Citrus Chicken Couscous

A hearty all-in-one supper but the citrus keeps it light. Use oranges or lemons, depending on what you have on hand, and add dried fruit to the couscous if you want a little more sweetness. Vegetarians can swap out the chicken for a small butternut squash cut into 2cm cubes and substitute vegetable stock for the chicken stock.

Serves 4–6

8 boneless, skinless chicken thighs
2 tbsp harissa
2 tbsp olive oil
½ tsp ground cinnamon
½ tsp fine sea salt
1 tbsp runny honey
3 large garlic cloves, finely chopped
2 oranges or lemons, washed and topped and tailed
2 red onions

for the couscous:
300g couscous
200g dried fruit such as sultanas, cranberries or chopped apricots (optional)
3 tbsp olive oil
1 tsp fine sea salt
500ml hot chicken stock
25g mint, chopped just before serving
25g coriander, chopped just before serving

Preheat the oven to 220°C/200°C fan. Cut each chicken thigh into three pieces. In a large bowl, combine the harissa, olive oil, cinnamon, salt, honey and garlic. Add the chicken and toss to coat. Cut the oranges or lemons into eighths, and peel and cut the red onions the same way. Arrange everything in a single layer in a large ovenproof dish and put into the oven while you prepare the couscous. Set a timer for 15 minutes.

Add the couscous to the now empty bowl that had the harissa in, add the dried fruit, if using, olive oil and salt, then pour over the hot stock. Give a stir, cover with a tea towel and set aside.

After 15 minutes of roasting, take the chicken out of the oven and give the dish a shake. Give the couscous a fluff with a fork, add it to the dish and mix together with the chicken. Return to the oven for another 20 minutes or until the couscous is golden. Remove from the oven, scatter over the chopped mint and coriander and serve straight from the dish.

Rosemary-Lemon Flat Iron Steak and Oven Chips

Flat iron is the chefs' secret cut – it's tender, very flavoursome and also great value. Served with hot chips this makes a delightfully simple supper that just needs a crisp green salad to complete it. For best results, rest your steak for 30 minutes at room temperature before you cook it.

Serves 4

800g flat iron steak, trimmed of sinew
1 tbsp olive oil
fine sea salt and freshly ground black pepper

50g butter, softened
2 garlic cloves, crushed
2 tbsp finely chopped rosemary
zest and 1 tbsp juice from 1 lemon
¼ tsp fine sea salt

for the oven chips:
750g large floury potatoes (Maris Piper, King Edward or Rooster work well), scrubbed and skin on
2 tbsp olive oil
½ tsp fine sea salt
1 tbsp cornflour
1 tsp paprika (optional)

Pat your steaks dry with kitchen paper and leave to come to room temperature. Preheat the oven to 240°C/220°C fan. Prepare a large bowl half-full of cold water. Cut the potatoes into long slices 1cm wide, then cut each slice into 1cm-wide chips. Put the raw chips in the cold water as you cut them so they don't discolour. Once they're all cut, drain them into a colander, rinse briefly, then pat dry thoroughly using a clean tea towel or paper towel. Dry your large bowl and use it to toss the chips with the olive oil, then salt, cornflour and paprika, if using. Line a large baking tray with greaseproof paper and arrange the chips on it in a single layer. Cover the baking tray with tin foil and bake for 10 minutes.

Meanwhile, mix the softened butter with the garlic, chopped rosemary, lemon zest and juice and salt in a small bowl and set it aside.

After the chips have had 10 minutes, remove the foil and return to the oven for another 20 minutes, making sure to flip them halfway through cooking.

Once the chips have gone back in the oven you can start to cook the steaks. Rub them with the olive oil and season well. Heat a large, cast-iron pan or sauté pan to very hot and add the steaks. Three minutes each side should give you medium rare and 4 minutes, medium. Check by cutting into one if you're not sure. Remove to a warm plate, and dot the rosemary-lemon butter over the top, then loosely cover with foil to rest for 10 to 12 minutes.

When ready to eat, slice the steaks across the grain into finger-width slices, then mix the steak juices with the melted butter on the plate and pour over them. Serve with the chips.

Borders are heavy with roses, and allotments brim with ripe tomatoes and basil and mint. This is the month of mists and mellow fruitfulness, of festivals, adventures and summer holidays.

tomatoes

field m

Aug

pineapple

Infallible Sesame Noodles with Peanut Sauce

So easy, and really delicious as a light supper with a colourful salad of julienned carrots and peppers. If you want to make it more substantial, add some grilled prawns or chicken. I make a full batch of this peanut sauce, even if I'm just cooking for myself, as it keeps well in a jar in the fridge and is handy for a fast noodle feast or as a delicious dip for Vietnamese Rice Paper Rolls (see p.45).

Serves 4

1 bunch spring onions
250g dried egg noodles or 500g udon noodles
1 lime, quartered, to serve

for the peanut sauce:
120g peanut butter (crunchy or smooth, your choice)
60ml (4 tbsp) tamari
2 tbsp toasted sesame seeds
3 tbsp rice vinegar
2 tbsp light sesame oil
2 tbsp runny honey
2 garlic cloves, peeled and grated
a thumb of fresh ginger, grated
1 tsp hot sauce

Top and tail the spring onions and slice them thinly lengthwise. Put them in a bowl of cold water and place in the fridge until you're ready to serve the noodles.

Then make the peanut sauce: in a medium bowl whisk together the peanut butter, tamari, toasted sesame seeds, rice vinegar, sesame oil, honey, grated garlic, ginger, hot sauce and 50ml hot water.

Cook the noodles according to the package instructions. Drain and rinse with cold water, then stir the noodles into the sauce until all are nicely coated.

Take the spring onions (which will have become curly) out of the fridge, drain them and arrange on top of the noodles, then serve with the wedges of lime on the side. Easy as that.

Bruschetta with Summer Tomatoes, Burrata and Basil

Enjoy as part of an antipasti platter or as the basis of a beautiful summer picnic. You can get creative with the toppings – another August favourite is chargrilled peaches, peppery rocket, and pistachios tossed in hot honey and salt (drop the garlic in that case). The homemade focaccia on p.139 works perfectly here, if you've got the time.

Serves 4–6

500g ripe tomatoes (cherry, plum or heirloom)
75ml olive oil
2 large garlic cloves, grated
4–8 slices of ciabatta, focaccia or sourdough
1 tbsp fresh lemon juice
15g basil, large stems removed
4 × 125g burrata
flaky sea salt and freshly ground black pepper

Halve the smaller tomatoes and core and cut any larger ones so all are a similar size. Place in a colander over a bowl (to catch the juice), add a pinch of salt, mix gently and set aside.

In a small pan, heat the olive oil and garlic over a very low heat for 3 to 4 minutes so the flavours infuse, then brush the slices of bread generously on one side with the garlicky oil. Heat a ribbed grill pan over a medium-high heat or use the grill of your oven and grill the bread until toasted and slightly charred on each side.

Make a dressing by mixing the lemon juice with the tomato juice collected from the chopped tomatoes and the remaining garlicky oil, then gently fold in the chopped tomatoes.

Arrange the tomatoes on a platter, tear over the basil and season well. Place the burratas on top and cut each one into pieces so the cream from them combines with the dressing. Serve on a platter and let people spoon the tomatoes onto their grilled bread themselves.

Crispy Coconut Prawns and Pineapple Salsa

There's something irresistible about crunchy prawns! This is a real summer holiday feast, with the zesty salsa bringing a touch of the tropical. Serve as shown or with some lettuce in a baguette to make a superior sandwich.

for the pineapple salsa:
300g ripe pineapple, cut into
   1cm cubes
15g fresh coriander, finely
   chopped
½ red onion, finely diced
1 red chilli, deseeded and
   finely chopped
1 tsp brown sugar
zest and juice of 1 lime
¼ tsp fine sea salt

for the mayo:
200g good quality mayo
1 tbsp Tabasco
1 garlic clove, grated
1 tbsp white wine vinegar

500g king prawns, shelled
70g self-raising flour
1 tsp fine sea salt
1 tsp freshly ground black
   pepper
1 egg white
75g fine desiccated coconut
50g panko
200ml sunflower oil for frying

Combine all the salsa ingredients in a bowl. In a separate bowl, combine all the mayo ingredients.

Pat the prawns dry with kitchen paper. Select three bowls and three forks. In the first bowl combine the flour and salt and pepper. In the second, put the egg white and give it a good whisk. In the third, mix the coconut and the panko. Line a baking tray with greaseproof paper and place it at the end of your row of bowls.

Heat the sunflower oil in a wok or large frying pan over a medium heat. Line a plate with kitchen paper and place it next to the stove along with tongs or a slotted spoon. Working in batches of three or four, dip the prawns into the flour, then the egg white and finally the coconut before laying them on the prepared baking tray.

When all the prawns are crumbed, fry them in batches of six and place them on the kitchen-paper-lined plate. They cook really quickly so keep an eye on them. If the oil's at the right temperature the prawns will take about 40 seconds on each side to become golden and crispy. Turn down the heat if they cook faster than that. Serve with the salsa and mayo.

Shawarma with Lemon and Garlic Potatoes

This is a simple method for making the most succulent shawarma you could ever hope to eat, and it works as wonderfully with mushrooms as it does with chicken. Serve with plenty of warm flatbreads (see p.138) to make this even more substantial.

Serves 4

for the shawarma marinade:
100ml extra virgin olive oil
juice of 1 lemon
3 garlic cloves, peeled
1 tsp dried oregano
1 tsp coriander seeds
1 tsp paprika or ½ tsp red
  chilli flakes
½ tsp ground cumin
½ tsp ground coriander
½ tsp fine sea salt
¼ tsp ground cinnamon

1 large onion
10 boneless, skinless
  chicken thighs, trimmed
  and flattened, or 12 large
  flat mushrooms such as
  portobello or field

for the garlic potatoes:
1kg baby potatoes
2 tbsp extra virgin olive oil
1 tsp fine sea salt
4–5 garlic cloves, skin left on
1 lemon, quartered, seeds
  removed
125g feta cheese

200g Greek yoghurt
15g flat-leaf parsley or
  coriander leaves, finely
  chopped

4 wooden skewers

Preheat the oven to 180°C/160°C fan. Blitz all the marinade ingredients together in a food processor or with a stick blender. If using chicken, add it to a large bowl with an additional ½ teaspoon of sea salt and the marinade and mix until well coated. If using mushrooms, wipe them clean and remove the stems (reserving them to roast with the potatoes). Put the mushroom tops in a large bowl with the marinade and mix until well coated.

Peel the onion, cut in half across and lay the halves flat-side down on a roasting tray. Stick two long skewers upright in each onion half, like flag poles, then push six mushrooms or five chicken thighs through the skewers on each onion so you have two tidy stacks. Cut the tops off the skewers so the stacks are easier to fit in the oven.

Cut the baby potatoes into halves or quarters so they're all a uniform size and add them to the bowl the marinade was in (with the reserved stems, if using mushrooms). Add the olive oil, salt, garlic and lemon quarters and mix so everything is well coated, then spread out on another rimmed baking tray. Put the shawarma on the top shelf of the oven, slide the potatoes in below and leave for 60 minutes, basting halfway through.

Mix the Greek yoghurt with half the chopped herbs and set aside. Take the shawarma out of the oven. Remove the roasted garlic from the potatoes, squeeze it into the herby yoghurt and mix. Add the pulp and juice from the roasted lemons to the potatoes (by squeezing against the back of a wooden spoon), then scatter with the rest of the chopped herbs and crumble over the feta. Slice the chicken or mushrooms down the length of the skewers and serve with the roast potatoes and the yoghurt dressing.

Lamb Koftas with Green Sauce

My friend and respected chef Canadian Al showed me the difference it makes to add hydrated breadcrumbs to koftas – it really keeps them light and juicy. I bake koftas because that's the easiest way to cook them but they can also be barbecued, grilled or fried in a heavy-bottomed pan. Serve with a big green salad, warm flatbreads (see p.138) and this amazingly tangy green sauce. If you've got time, make some Chilli Crisp as well (see p.136).

Serves 4

2 tbsp harissa
75g dry breadcrumbs or panko
500g minced Scottish lamb
1 large shallot, finely chopped
1 large egg, beaten
2 garlic cloves, grated
1 tsp ground cumin
1 tsp ground coriander
¼ tsp ground cinnamon
1 tsp fine sea salt
1 tbsp olive oil

for the green sauce:
15g coriander
30g mint, leaves only
zest and juice of 1 lime
3–4 tbsp olive oil

2 tbsp harissa or Chilli Crisp (p.136)
300g Greek yoghurt

Preheat your oven to 200°C/180°C fan. In a large bowl, mix the harissa with 50ml water, then stir in the breadcrumbs or panko and set aside for 5 minutes while they hydrate. Add the lamb, shallot, egg, garlic, cumin, coriander, cinnamon and salt and incorporate – I find squishing with my hands the most effective way to do this. Now divide the mixture into eight equal pieces and shape into either cigar-sausages, the best shape for filling a flatbread, or little patties if you have rolls.

Line a roasting dish with greaseproof paper, arrange the koftas on top and drizzle with the olive oil. Bake on the top shelf of the oven, turning halfway through cooking, until brown and cooked all the way through, about 18 to 20 minutes.

Meanwhile, throw together the sauces: blitz the coriander, mint, lime zest and juice and olive oil in a food processor to make the green sauce, and simply swirl the harissa or Chilli Crisp through the yoghurt in a bowl. Take to the table so everyone can help themselves.

August's hot pinks and dusty yellows turn into crimson and gold as the Earth tilts and the warmth of summer subsides. Fresh thoughts, cool air, new pencils and woolly socks to tame wild seaside bare toes. Low sun makes long shadows that stretch into evenings and we start to feel the big dark sky. Figs, pistachios, pilafs and pies make for happy suppers; we savour the flavours just as we relish the long rays of the sun when they find us.

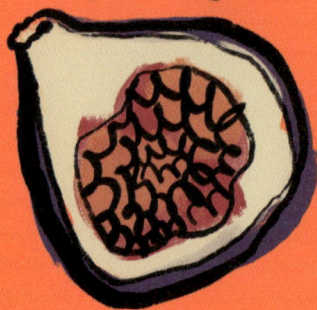
fig

chives

Septe

leek

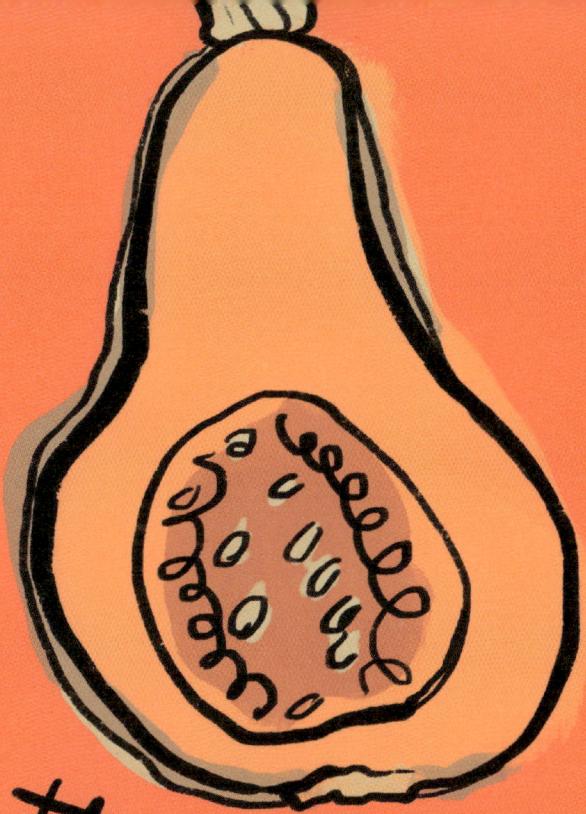
butternut squash

mber

Caramelised Onion Galette with Manchego, Fresh Figs and Thyme

From scratch this is a relaxed weekend project. For weeknight simplicity use premade and pre-rolled shortcrust pastry. The caramelised onions can be made up to 3 days in advance to save time too.

September

Serves 4

for the pastry:
250g plain flour, plus a little extra for dusting
150g cold butter, cut into small cubes
½ tsp fine sea salt
6–7 tbsp ice-cold water

2 tbsp olive oil
4 medium red onions, peeled and thinly sliced
2 large garlic cloves, thinly sliced
1 tbsp balsamic vinegar
1 tsp brown sugar
5 sprigs thyme or lemon thyme
1 tbsp wholegrain mustard
150g manchego (rind cut off)
1 egg yolk
3 ripe figs, quartered
1 tbsp runny honey
sea salt and freshly ground black pepper

To make the pastry, put the flour, butter and salt into the bowl of a food processor and pulse until the butter is incorporated into the flour. Add the ice-cold water a spoonful at a time, lightly pulsing in between to mix, until it comes together into a ball. You may not need all the water. Tip the dough onto a floured surface, dust the top with flour and flatten into a thick disc shape, then wrap in greaseproof or cling film and refrigerate.

Heat the olive oil in a large sauté pan over a medium heat and add the sliced onions. Cook for 4 to 5 minutes, until the onions have softened, then lower the heat and stir in the garlic, balsamic, brown sugar and the leaves from three of the sprigs of thyme. Cook for another 15 to 20 minutes, stirring occasionally, until everything is softened and has turned a burnished gold colour.

Preheat your oven to 200°C/180°C fan. Lightly flour a sheet of greaseproof, place the dough on it and roll out into a circle about 40cm in diameter. Slide the greaseproof onto a baking sheet. Place the mustard in the centre of the pastry and use the back of a spoon to spread it into a large circle, leaving a 5cm border around the edges. Grate 100g of the manchego and stir that into the caramelised onions, then spoon the onions onto the dough and spread them out over the mustard. Season liberally, then fold the uncovered edges up and over the onions to contain them.

Whisk the egg yolk with a splash of water and a pinch of salt and brush over the exposed pastry. Transfer the galette, still on the baking sheet, into the hot oven and bake for 30 to 35 minutes, or until the pastry is golden.

When the finished galette has cooled a little, arrange the quartered figs on top and shave over the remaining manchego. Drizzle over the honey, scatter with the leaves from the remaining two sprigs of thyme and serve.

Spiced Butternut Pilaf

This is a really tasty way to enjoy this season's squash – roasting brings out its delicious sweetness and dried fruit and nuts add to the autumnal flavours.

Serves 4

100g almonds, hazelnuts, pistachios or walnuts, sliced

500g butternut squash (half of a medium-sized one), peeled

2 tbsp olive oil

½ tsp allspice

1 medium red onion, finely chopped

a thumb of ginger, peeled and finely chopped

3 garlic cloves, grated

300g jasmine or basmati rice

700ml vegetable stock

150g dried cherries, cranberries or raisins

fine sea salt and freshly ground black pepper

You'll need a large saucepan, casserole or sauté pan with a tight-fitting lid. Over a medium heat, toast the nuts in the pan until they are golden, then remove to a plate and set aside.

Chop the squash into approximately 15mm cubes, add to a large bowl and toss with the olive oil, allspice and some salt and pepper until well coated. Transfer to your pan and sauté over a medium heat for 4 to 5 minutes. Add the onion and ginger and continue to cook until the onion has softened, about 3 to 4 minutes, then add the garlic. Stir well to incorporate, then add the rice, stirring for a minute or so to toast the grains and coat them in the oil. Turn up the heat a little and add the stock, then stir in the dried fruit and the toasted nuts and put the lid on the pan. Let the stock come to a simmer, then turn the heat to low and cook for 15 minutes. Take the pan off the heat and leave with the lid firmly in place for another 10 minutes to let the rice steam before serving.

Fish Pie

You can fine-tune this to your liking: leave out the eggs, try different herbs or put Gruyère in the mash. Too much smoked haddock is a bit overwhelming but one is just right.

Serves 4

for the mash:
butter for greasing
1kg floury potatoes (Maris Piper, Rooster or Desiree are all good)
100g butter, fridge cold
25g chives, finely chopped
zest of 1 lemon
fine sea salt and freshly ground black pepper

4 large eggs (optional)

for the filling:
500ml whole milk
1 bay leaf
750g fish made up of skinless hake, salmon, smoked haddock, cod (all cut into roughly 3cm pieces), king prawns (shelled, deveined and left whole)
30g butter
1 medium leek, white part only, finely sliced
30g plain flour
100g fresh or frozen peas
fine sea salt and freshly ground black pepper

Preheat your oven to 220°C/200°C fan. Butter an ovenproof dish (approx. 22 × 28cm) and place it on a baking tray. Peel and dice the potatoes, then simmer in well-salted water until tender. Drain and set aside in a colander. If you're adding eggs to the filling, boil them for 10 minutes then cool in cold water and peel.

Make the filling. Bring the milk and bay leaf to a simmer in a large pan. Add the fish, bring back to a simmer, then cook for 3 minutes. Turn off the heat and, using a slotted spoon to drain the fish well, transfer it to the buttered baking dish. Keep the milk in the pan.

Melt the 30g butter in a large frying pan, add the finely sliced leeks and season. Cook over a gentle heat until very tender and fragrant, about 5 minutes. Then sprinkle in the flour, stirring, and cook for 2 minutes. Continue stirring and slowly add the warm milk ladle by ladle. Bring to the boil, then reduce the heat to low and stir until the sauce thickens to the consistency of double cream, about 5 to 6 minutes.

Scatter the peas over the fish in the dish, quarter the boiled eggs, if using, and arrange them in a layer, then pour the sauce over everything. Lastly, grate the 100g of cold butter over the cooked potatoes and mash up. Stir in the chives and lemon zest and season well. Spoon the mash over the fish and comb into an even layer using a fork, then place in the oven for 20 minutes or until the pie is golden and the sauce is bubbling at the edges.

Tarragon and Crème Fraîche Chicken

There's something undeniably elegant about this dish. This is a supper to light the candles for. It's so bistro, so simple, so delicious!

Serves 4

8 chicken thighs, bone-in, skin-on
20g butter
1 tbsp olive oil
2 medium shallots, finely chopped
3 garlic cloves, finely chopped
150ml white wine
1 tbsp Dijon mustard
150ml chicken stock, fresh or from a gel pot
200g crème fraîche
20g tarragon, stalks removed, leaves roughly chopped
fine sea salt and freshly ground black pepper

Pat the chicken thighs dry with kitchen paper and season well with ½ teaspoon of salt and plenty of freshly ground black pepper.

In a large sauté pan or frying pan, melt the butter with the oil over a medium heat and add the chicken thighs skin-side down. If you can't fit them in a single layer, fry them in batches. Leave the chicken to render and crisp, without touching it, for 10 to 12 minutes. Use tongs to turn the chicken over and cook for another 10 minutes. When the thighs are fully cooked the juices will run clear rather than pink when pierced with a sharp knife. Remove from the pan to a large plate.

Keep the pan on the heat and add the shallots and garlic and soften them, stirring occasionally, for 3 to 4 minutes. Turn up the heat a little and add the white wine, stirring again to loosen and incorporate any browned, crispy bits in the pan. The wine will begin to simmer straight away and then reduce. After 3 minutes stir in the mustard, then the stock, crème fraîche and chopped tarragon. Bring to a steady simmer, then return the chicken to the pan along with its juices from the plate. Lower the heat, put the lid on and simmer for another 5 to 10 minutes before serving with French beans and new potatoes.

Rosy apples and rosy cheeks as the cold starts to nip. This is the month that the curtain falls and fingers of frost start to freeze cobwebs. The rare sun feels like a gift when it turns autumn trees into monuments of colour. We seek comfort in the warm kitchen – making the time for satisfying stews and hearty pasta dishes.

aubergine

Octo

celery

red
apple

cabbage

ober

Hearty Tuscan Bean Stew

I've allowed generous quantities here as people always come back for seconds, even thirds. If your mob are more restrained, this freezes like a dream or can be Phoenixed back to life as 'bean soup' with the addition of another can of crushed tomatoes and scatterings of chopped basil and Parmesan. Serve with hot focaccia (see p.139) or a big steaming bowl of pasta and lots of black pepper.

October

Serves 4

2 tbsp olive oil

1 medium onion, finely diced

2 medium carrots, peeled and finely diced

2 stalks celery, finely diced

4 garlic cloves, finely chopped

1 tbsp tomato paste

150ml red wine

3 × 400g tins beans such as borlotti, butter or cannellini (any combo you like), drained and rinsed

400g tin Italian plum tomatoes or 400g passata

¼ tsp chilli flakes

a pinch of sugar

300ml vegetable stock

5 sprigs of thyme

1 bay leaf

1 tsp extra virgin olive oil

1 tbsp orange juice from the zested orange (below)

1 tsp flaky sea salt

100g cavolo nero or curly kale, thick stems removed, leaves finely chopped

fine sea salt and freshly ground black pepper

to serve:

zest of 1 small orange

2 sprigs of rosemary

Add the olive oil to a large, heavy-bottomed saucepan over a medium heat. When hot, add the onion, carrots and celery and cook, stirring occasionally, until softened, about 5 to 6 minutes. Add the garlic and cook for another minute. Stir in the tomato paste and turn up the heat a little so the tomatoey veg brown and almost start to catch on the bottom of the pan.

Add the red wine, stir well and simmer until reduced by about half. Then add the beans, tomatoes or passata, chilli flakes, sugar, a decent pinch of salt and a few grinds of black pepper and bring back to a simmer. Add the vegetable stock, thyme sprigs and bay leaf. Simmer, without a lid, until thickened, about 20 to 25 minutes.

Meanwhile pick the rosemary leaves, finely chop them and mix with the orange zest. Set this aside.

In a large bowl mix the extra virgin olive oil, the orange juice and the salt and add the finely chopped cavolo nero or kale, massaging the dressing into the leaves with your fingertips.

Fold the greens into the hot beans 2 minutes before serving. Taste and adjust the seasoning to your liking, then take the stew to the table and finish with a sprinkle of the rosemary-orange mixture.

Spicy Aubergine Rigatoni

Aubergine at its most irresistible – roasted in spices and lightened with tangy crème fraîche. Take it to the next level by serving it with Walnut Salsa (see p.137).

Serves 4

2 tbsp olive oil
1 tsp miso
1 tsp fennel seeds
½ tsp chilli flakes
2–3 medium aubergines, halved lenthways
15g flat-leaf parsley or marjoram leaves, finely chopped
200ml crème fraîche
500g good quality rigatoni
fine sea salt and freshly ground black pepper

Preheat the oven to 200°C/180°C fan. Add the olive oil, miso, fennel seeds, chilli flakes and ¼ teaspoon of salt to a medium bowl and mix well.

Line a rimmed baking tray or roasting dish with greaseproof paper and arrange the aubergine halves cut-side up. Use a sharp knife to mark a criss-cross pattern into each aubergine half, taking care not to puncture the skin, and paint the spiced oil onto the open faces (set the oily bowl aside for later). Then flip the aubergines so they're skin-side up, put the tray into the oven and roast for 20 to 25 minutes or until completely tender and fragrant.

Remove the aubergines from the oven and drain in a colander or sieve over a bowl for 2 to 3 minutes, pressing gently to get rid of any excess moisture. Scrape the flesh from the skins into the bowl that contained the spiced oil. Reserving a pinch for a garnish, add the chopped parsley or marjoram to the bowl and mix in along with the crème fraiche, then season to taste.

Cook the pasta according to the packet instructions, drain, then stir through the spicy aubergine, garnish with the reserved parsley or marjoram and serve.

Kedgeree

Although it's traditionally a breakfast dish, I find kedgeree to be one of the loveliest quick suppers – light, spicy and satisfying. If you can't find smoked haddock, Arbroath smokies or hot smoked salmon also make stellar kedgeree.

Serves 4

300g basmati rice, rinsed well

zest and juice of 1 lemon

1 tsp turmeric

½ tsp fine sea salt

10–20g butter (optional)

600ml vegetable stock or water

4 eggs

450g smoked haddock (preferably undyed)

1 tbsp olive oil

25g butter

1 medium onion, finely chopped

a small thumb of fresh ginger, peeled and finely chopped

2 tsp garam masala

10g flat-leaf parsley leaves, chopped

15g chives, finely chopped

fine sea salt and freshly ground black pepper

Place the rice, lemon zest, turmeric, salt, butter, if using, and stock or water in a medium saucepan and bring to the boil over a medium heat. Reduce the heat a little and simmer, covered, for 12 minutes, then remove from the heat and leave covered for 10 minutes while you prepare the rest of the kedgeree.

Place the eggs in a small pan (that has a lid) and cover with cold water, add a pinch of salt and bring to the boil. As soon as the water boils, turn off the heat, put the lid on the pan and set aside. Ten to 15 minutes will give you hard-boiled eggs. Drain and cool them under cold running water when ready to peel them.

Half fill a large frying pan with water and bring to a simmer. Add the fish skin-side up and cook for 8 minutes, then drain and break into large flakes. Discard the skin. Keep the fish warm on a plate covered with foil while you heat the olive oil and butter in the frying pan. Add the onion and ginger and soften for 5 to 6 minutes, then add the lemon juice and garam masala and cook for 2 to 3 minutes. Gently add the fish back to the pan, stirring so you don't break it up, then carefully fold in the rice, a big spoonful at a time. Peel and halve the boiled eggs and arrange on top, then scatter over the chopped parsley and chives before serving.

Pretzel Chicken with Apple Slaw

Salty pretzels make a surprisingly tasty and crispy crust for fried chicken, while buttermilk keeps the meat succulent. Substitute natural yoghurt if you can't find buttermilk. The chicken breast is butterflied so it's half as thick and twice as wide – making it a great vehicle for a crispy coating!

Serves 4

for the apple slaw:
100g cavolo nero,
   de-stemmed
¼ red cabbage
2 tbsp extra virgin olive oil
2 tbsp apple cider vinegar
1 tsp Dijon mustard
1 garlic clove, grated
2 apples
1 stalk celery, finely sliced
50g pecans or walnuts,
   roughly chopped
50g dried cranberries

300ml buttermilk
1 tbsp Dijon mustard
1 garlic clove, crushed
1 tsp thyme (dried or
   chopped fresh)
1 tsp paprika
½ tsp fine sea salt
150g small, salted pretzels
4 skinless, boneless chicken
   breasts
200ml sunflower oil
2 tbsp maple syrup
juice of 1 lemon
   (approx. 2 tbsp)

Finely chop the cavolo nero and red cabbage and put in a large salad bowl. Add ½ tablespoon of the olive oil and use your fingertips to massage it into the leaves to soften them. In a separate bowl, whisk together the remaining 1½ tablespoons of olive oil and the vinegar, mustard and garlic. Core the apples, finely slice them and add to the kale with the celery, pecans or walnuts and the cranberries. Add the dressing and toss to combine.

In a large shallow bowl, mix the buttermilk, mustard, garlic, thyme, paprika and salt. Blitz the pretzels in a food processor until fine crumbs, then tip into a large, rimmed baking tray.

Butterfly the chicken: simply cut in half across the whole breast, stopping short a centimetre before you cut in half completely, then bash to flatness between two pieces of greaseproof paper. Dip each piece of chicken into the buttermilk, give a little shake, then lay on the pretzel crumb and turn over to make sure it's covered completely.

Heat the sunflower oil in a large, heavy-bottomed frying pan over a medium-high heat. Once the oil is shimmering and hot enough that a drop of buttermilk sizzles when added to the pan, add a piece of chicken and cook until the crust is golden brown and the chicken is cooked through, 3 to 5 minutes per side. Transfer to a kitchen-paper-lined plate and keep warm while you repeat the process with the remaining chicken.

Whisk together the maple syrup and lemon juice and transfer to a little jug or bowl. Serve the chicken with a drizzle of the lemon maple syrup and mounds of the green apple slaw.

Roast Gnocchi with Sausages, Apples and Shallots

Any kind of sausage will work well here, including veggie or vegan. If you're using Italian sausages with chilli and fennel, it's nice to add fennel seeds and ½ teaspoon of dried chilli flakes into the mix.

250g Cumberland sausages, casings removed
500g potato gnocchi
6 small shallots, peeled and halved
3 garlic cloves, unpeeled
3 tbsp extra virgin olive oil
100ml white wine or veg stock
2 Cox's Orange Pippin apples, cored and cut into thick slices
100g baby spinach, washed
1 tbsp finely chopped rosemary (optional)
fine sea salt and freshly ground black pepper

for the dressing:
1 tbsp wholegrain mustard
1 tbsp apple cider vinegar
1 tsp runny honey
1 tbsp extra virgin olive oil

Preheat your oven to 220°C/200°C fan. Line a large, rimmed roasting tray or ovenproof dish with greaseproof paper. Pull or roughly chop the sausage meat into gnocchi-sized pieces and put in a large mixing bowl. Add the gnocchi, shallots, garlic, olive oil and wine or stock. Season well and toss together until coated.

Tip the mixture onto the tray, give it a shake so everything's in a single layer, and put in the oven for 15 minutes. Take the tray out of the oven, scatter over the apple slices, and give another shake to flip everything a bit for even cooking. Roast for another 15 minutes, or until the sausage and gnocchi are browning and cooked through and the shallots are tender. Five minutes before everything is done, make the dressing by mixing together the mustard, vinegar, honey and olive oil.

Take the tray out of the oven, pick out the garlic cloves and squeeze them out into your dressing, using a fork to mash and incorporate them. Mix the baby spinach into the hot ingredients so it wilts a little and drizzle over the dressing. Finally, sprinkle over the chopped rosemary, if using, and serve.

The clocks have not long turned back an hour, giving us jet lag in the most pedestrian way. November is a festival of roots, spices, pies and braises, bringing warmth and sustaining richness. We bolster ourselves with fire festivals, get-togethers and dishes celebrating the best of the season, like plump mussels from cold, clear waters and brisket cooked with red wine.

shal

mussels

Nove

ts

cauliflower

mber

Cauliflower Croque Monsieur

A creative twist on the classic French sandwich. I like to customise it even further by using Isle of Mull Cheddar and wholegrain mustard from Arran, but feel free to use whatever you have on hand. Put any cauliflower offcuts in the pan when you roast the slices – they're delicious in a leafy salad, and you can use the juice from the zested lemon to make a dressing.

Serves 4

1 large cauliflower
2 tbsp olive oil
½ tsp garlic powder
zest of 1 lemon
160g crème fraîche
3 egg yolks
300g Emmenthal, Gruyère or mature Cheddar, finely grated
4 tsp mustard such as Dijon, honey or wholegrain
200g best-quality cooked, sliced ham
fine sea salt and freshly ground black pepper

Preheat the oven 230°C/210°C fan. Line a baking sheet with greaseproof paper. Slice the cauliflower into four slices each a thumb-width (about 2cm) thick. Mix the oil, garlic powder and lemon zest in a small bowl and brush over the cauliflower slices so they are entirely coated, then season liberally on both sides with about ½ teaspoon of salt and a teaspoon of black pepper. Any loose cauliflower pieces can be drizzled with olive oil and added to the baking sheet to roast too. Roast the cauliflower steaks in the oven for 15 minutes on one side.

Meanwhile, make your croque top by whisking together the crème fraîche and egg yolks and stirring in the grated cheese and plenty of seasoning.

When the cauliflower is done on the first side, turn the slices over and roast for 10 minutes on the other side, then remove from the oven and spread a teaspoon of mustard over each slice, top with some ham and then 2 to 3 tablespoons of the crème fraîche mixture. Place back in the oven for 10 minutes or until the tops are melted, golden and bubbling.

Mussels with White Wine, Crème Fraîche and Parsley

Work in batches if your pan isn't big enough – or use a wok with a flat baking tray for a lid, which has worked well for me in the past. Serve with crusty bread and many napkins.

Serves 4

2kg Scottish mussels, from a fishmonger
2 tbsp extra virgin olive oil
2 shallots, finely chopped
2 garlic cloves, grated
200ml dry white wine
150g crème fraîche
30g flat-leaf parsley, picked from thickest stems and finely chopped

Fill your sink with cold water and put the mussels in. Remove any barnacles with the back of a table knife, pull off any weedy beards at the hinge end and discard any open mussels that don't close when you tap them.

In a lidded pan large enough to comfortably hold all the mussels, heat the olive oil over a medium heat and add the shallots, then after 4 to 5 minutes add the garlic. Add the white wine and bring to a boil, then add the mussels and give the pan a good shake to coat them all in the liquid. Now clamp the lid on and steam for 5 minutes or until all the mussels have opened. Remove the mussels to a large bowl or bowls, leaving the broth in the pan. Whisk the crème fraîche and chopped parsley into the broth, then pour it over the mussels and tuck in.

Coq au Vin

The classic French chicken stew, perfect with rice, boiled potatoes or a crusty baguette. This might be even better the day after it's been made, if you're a planner.

Serves 4–6

8 bone-in, skin-on chicken thighs

150g lardons or 4 slices thick-cut streaky bacon, cut into strips

1 tbsp olive oil

3 carrots, peeled and sliced on the diagonal

5 small shallots, peeled (halved if bigger than your thumb)

250g chestnut mushrooms, brushed and halved

3 garlic cloves, sliced

2 tbsp plain flour

2 tbsp tomato paste

350ml light, fruity red wine (ideally a Burgundy such as Pinot Noir)

350ml good-quality chicken stock

3 sprigs of thyme

2 bay leaves

30g flat-leaf parsley, leaves chopped, some reserved to garnish

fine sea salt and freshly ground black pepper

Season the chicken thighs with plenty of salt and pepper. Place a large casserole (that has a lid) over a medium heat, add the bacon while the pan is still cold and bring it up to heat, stirring occasionally, until it has browned and much of its fat has rendered and covers the base of the casserole. Remove the bacon, leaving the fat in the pan, and add the thighs, four at a time, to brown on each side. Set aside on a deepish plate to catch the juices.

Preheat the oven to 180°C/160°C fan. Add the olive oil to your pan, then add the carrots, shallots and mushrooms and sauté for 3 to 5 minutes over a medium heat, stirring occasionally, until golden. Stir in the garlic and a pinch of salt and cook for another minute or so. Add the flour and the tomato paste and, using a wooden spoon, mix well so that all the veg are coated. The paste will cling to the veg and start to brown quite quickly. Before the veg start to burn, add the wine, stirring to help dislodge all the brown bits from the bottom of the casserole. Add the chicken stock, the browned thighs and the thyme, bay leaves and parsley, keeping the heat high until the stock starts to boil. Then turn the heat down, put the lid on the casserole and place in the oven for 40 to 45 minutes. When it's done, scatter over the reserved chopped parsley and serve at the table.

Crofter's Pie

Haggis is a really wintery treat, rich and spicy, making it perfect to put in a pie. Vegetarian haggis works just as well as a straight swap here. Serve with mountains of sweet boiled and mashed neeps or roast celeriac for a hearty supper on a cold, dark night.

Serves 4–6

for the mash:

4 large floury potatoes
(approx. 500g), peeled

50ml milk

30g butter

20g fresh chives, finely
chopped (optional)

fine sea salt and freshly
ground black pepper

for the pie:

2 onions, finely diced

2 medium carrots, finely
diced

1 tbsp demerara sugar

1 garlic clove, crushed

1 tsp fresh thyme leaves

500g traditional or
vegetarian haggis, skin
removed and haggis
chopped

500ml beef, chicken or veg
stock

1 tsp cornflour, combined
with a little water to form
a paste

150g fresh or frozen peas

50ml whisky (optional)

fine sea salt and freshly
ground pepper

Preheat the oven to 180°C/160°C fan. Cut the potatoes into even-sized pieces, place in a large pan, cover with cold water and add a teaspoon of salt. Boil until the potatoes are tender, about 12 to 15 minutes, then drain and leave to dry in a colander.

Meanwhile, fry the onions and carrots, stirring, for about 5 minutes or until soft and golden. Sprinkle over the sugar and ¼ teaspoon of salt and cook for another 5 minutes, stirring constantly, then add the garlic and fresh thyme and cook for a further 2 to 3 minutes. Add the chopped haggis to the onion mixture and stir to incorporate. Add the hot stock and cornflour paste and simmer for about 10 minutes, then add the peas and the whisky, if using. Taste and correct seasoning if it needs it, then decant into your pie dish.

The potatoes will have steamed dry by now. Mash them with the milk and butter and add the chives, if using. Then season generously with salt and freshly ground black pepper and spread it over the haggis in your pie dish. Bake in the oven for about 20 minutes, until the craggy mash has golden peaks and the haggis mixture is bubbling at the sides.

Brisket

A wide casserole with a lid is perfect for braising brisket. You could also use a roasting pan with a couple of layers of tin foil pinched around the edges to seal it. If your roasting tin doesn't have a heavy base, sear the brisket and veg in a frying pan first and decant into the roasting dish to braise. Serve with mashed potatoes and lots of steamed broccoli and green beans.

50g flaky sea salt

2 tbsp very finely chopped rosemary

2 tsp garlic powder

1 tbsp sweet paprika

1 tsp black pepper, finely ground

1 tbsp orange or lemon zest

1.5–2kg beef brisket, trimmed of fat and silverskin

1 tbsp sunflower oil

3 medium carrots, peeled and cut into 4 on the diagonal

2 medium onions, peeled and quartered

1 bulb of garlic, cut across the equator

300ml red wine or Buckfast

100g fresh ginger, peeled and cut into discs the thickness of a pound coin

500ml beef stock (hands-down best is from Truefoods – keep it in the freezer for everything!!)

1 tbsp brown sugar or honey

1 tbsp cornflour, combined with a little water to form a paste

Preheat your oven to 160°C/140°C fan. Make the rub by mixing the salt, rosemary, garlic powder, sweet paprika, black pepper and orange or lemon zest together in a bowl. Rub the brisket all over with sunflower oil, then sprinkle over the rub mix and massage it in. Leave to stand while you prepare the rest of the ingredients.

Get your pan hot over a medium heat, then sear the brisket on each side. This should take 5 to 6 minutes; you want a really good golden crust to form but you don't want to burn the seasoning. Remove to a large plate and add the carrots, onions and garlic to the pan. Allow them to colour and caramelise a bit at the edges, about 4 or 5 minutes.

Add the red wine or Buckfast and, with a wooden spoon, make sure all the browned, crispy bits of beef and vegetables stuck to the bottom of the pan are dislodged. Now add the ginger, beef stock and the brown sugar. When the brown sugar has dissolved into the broth and everything is gently simmering, rest the beef on the vegetables, put the lid on the pan and put into the oven for 1 hour per 500g of beef. Check after 4 hours. It should be tender enough to cut like butter. To serve, remove the meat to a plate and use a slotted spoon to remove the veg from the broth. To make an easy gravy, add the cornflour paste to the broth and whisk in while it simmers on the hob. Slice your brisket across the grain and add back into the gravy.

Here is December with its dark glittering skies. We use fairy lights to bring the stars inside, citrus to put the sunshine into our food and herbs to bring fragrance. Dark leafy greens fortify us at this time of year, and we share feasts like roast chicken prepared in a flash or delicious salmon baked in a buttery pastry crust. Even Orion might loosen his belt.

celeria

Dece

Brussels sprouts

rosemary

mber

St Clements Brussels Sprouts with Garlicky Puy Lentils

I crave this smoky citrus combo in the winter months. It makes the perfect supper (with a fried egg on it if you're feeling lush) or serve it as a special occasion side dish. Puy lentils are so easy and so satisfyingly filling.

Serves 4

250g Puy (green) lentils
3 garlic cloves, lightly crushed
30ml extra virgin olive oil
500g Brussels sprouts, outer leaves removed
1 medium leek, white and light green part only
150g smoked pancetta or vegetarian bacon, cut into 5mm cubes
20g salted butter
2 garlic cloves, grated
zest of 1 lemon
zest of ½ orange
10g flat-leaf parsley, finely chopped
50g pine nuts, toasted
fine sea salt and freshly ground black pepper

Rinse the lentils and put in a pan with plenty of cold water and the garlic and bring to a simmer. Cook for 20 to 25 minutes, until the lentils are tender but still firm. Drain, discarding the garlic, and mix with the olive oil and ¼ teaspoon fine sea salt. Keep warm until ready to serve.

Meanwhile, quarter the Brussels sprouts, and halve the leek lengthwise, then finely slice it into half-moons. Heat a large sauté pan or non-stick frying pan over a medium heat, add the pancetta and sauté for 2 to 3 minutes, until it starts to turn golden. For vegetarian bacon, add 1 teaspoon olive oil and cook for 1 to 2 minutes.

When the pancetta or bacon is golden, add the butter and let it sizzle, then add the leeks and the sprouts and stir well to incorporate. Sauté until bright green and tender, about 5 to 6 minutes. Add the garlic, lemon and orange zests, finely chopped parsley and pine nuts, and sauté for another minute until fragrant. Check and adjust the seasoning and serve over the warm Puy lentils.

Salmon en Croute with Lemon Thyme

This is one for a weekend or a small celebration buffet. Use a good-quality cream cheese such as Philadelphia as inferior brands can be watery. To make it Christmassy, add the zest of an orange and a handful or two of dried cranberries to the herb mix. Delish!

Serves 4 (or 6–8 as part of a buffet)

zest of 1 lemon

1 tbsp chopped lemon thyme

1 tsp garlic powder

600–700g salmon fillet, skinned, belly fat trimmed and pin-boned

25g basil, thick stems discarded

25g dill

25g chives

50g watercress, thick stems discarded

2 egg yolks

280g good-quality cream cheese

2 × 320g ready-rolled puff pastry sheets (made with butter)

sea salt and freshly ground black pepper

Mix the lemon zest, thyme, garlic powder, a teaspoon of salt and a tablespoon of black pepper together to make a rub. Pat the salmon dry with kitchen paper and sprinkle the rub all over.

Finely chop the herbs and watercress and add to a large bowl with one of the egg yolks, the cream cheese, a pinch of salt and a good grind of black pepper, and mix.

Whisk the other egg yolk with a tablespoon of water and ¼ teaspoon of salt. Line a large, rimmed baking tray with greaseproof paper and lay a sheet of pastry on it. Lay the seasoned salmon fillet in the centre, then brush some egg wash over the pastry around the salmon, keeping the rest of it aside for later.

Preheat the oven to 220°C/200°C fan. Spread the cream cheese mix over the salmon in an even layer, then lay the other pastry sheet over the top. Press the top layer of pastry gently down around the salmon and then, leaving a 2 to 3cm rim, cut the excess pastry away with a knife, and reserve the pastry trimmings. Use a fork to press the edges of the two sheets together to seal them. Cut two holes so the steam can escape, then use the leftover pastry trimmings to make shapes to decorate the parcel. Brush with the remaining egg wash and bake in the oven for 25 to 30 minutes, until the pastry is golden and puffed. Allow to rest uncovered for at least 15 minutes before serving.

Lemon Roast Spatchcock Chicken

It's easy to spatchcock a chicken and it dramatically reduces the cooking time. The onion and lemon slices here prevent the chicken burning on the bottom and also yield the most delicious gravy. Serve with Wonderful Fries (see p.138) and a leafy salad, gravy on the side.

Serves 4–6

1.4–1.8kg best-quality free-range chicken

1 lemon

1 tbsp finely chopped rosemary, or 2 tsp dried rosemary

2 tsp garlic powder

5 tbsp olive oil

2 medium onions

100ml white or rosé wine, or stock, if you prefer

fine sea salt and freshly ground black pepper

Place the chicken breast-side down on your chopping board. Using a pair of sturdy scissors, cut along each side of the backbone and remove it. Turn the chicken over so it's breast-side up and press it firmly with the palm of your hand to flatten it out. Thoroughly pat it dry with kitchen paper, then season all over with 2 teaspoons each of salt and pepper. Zest the lemon and mix with the rosemary, garlic powder and olive oil in a bowl, then rub into the chicken on both sides.

Preheat the oven to 220°C/190°C fan. Peel and cut the onions into 1cm-thick slices and slice the lemon the same way, then scatter the slices over the base of the roasting tin and rest the seasoned chicken on top, skin-side up. Roast for approximately 45 minutes, but after 20 minutes add the wine or stock, basting it gently over the chicken. Don't pour the liquid directly over the chicken when you add it because that will stop the skin getting crispy.

The chicken is ready when the juices run clear when it's pierced at the leg and the joints are loose and pull apart easily. Let it rest out of the oven, loosely covered with foil, for 10 to 15 minutes. The juices in the bottom of the pan will have made a delicious, light gravy.

Barley Risotto with Cider and Bacon

Always al dente, nutty barley is delicious but also so good for you. It's high in iron so can help prevent anaemia and fatigue, and it contains selenium, which can help preserve skin elasticity. It's also an excellent source of fibre. I just love it. This goes just as beautifully with a salad as it does with sausages or Sunday's roast chicken.

Serves 4

1 tbsp olive oil or 15g butter

150g smoked streaky bacon or smoked pancetta, cut into cubes or strips (optional)

1 large leek, halved, sliced thinly, then washed

1 carrot, chopped

250g swede or celeriac, cut into 1cm cubes

350g pearl barley

300ml dry cider

1l hot vegetable or chicken stock

1 tsp chopped flat-leaf parsley

1 tsp chopped rosemary or sage

salt and freshly ground black pepper

Heat the olive oil or butter in a large pot over a medium heat, add the bacon or pancetta and fry gently for 2 to 3 minutes, until it begins to brown. Add the leek, carrot, swede or celeriac and barley, and stir until everything is coated in the oil and the veg start to tenderise, about 5 to 6 minutes. Now turn up the heat a bit so everything sizzles and add the cider, then lower the heat and simmer until the liquid has reduced by about half.

Add the hot stock next – all at once – and let it simmer, stirring occasionally, until the barley has plumped and most of the liquid has been absorbed, about 40 minutes. Stir in the finely chopped herbs for the last few minutes of simmering. Finally, taste and adjust the seasoning, making sure to add plenty of freshly ground black pepper.

Delicious Additions

It's always good to be able to whip up a delicious sauce, salsa or dressing – a little flavour boost can lift a dish to new heights. Here are a selection of my favourite accompaniments, along with some incredibly handy recipes for fries and quick breads.

Chilli Crisp

Store in a clean jar in the fridge until you need a flavour grenade. Keeps for up to a month.

55g whole, Chinese dried chillies
55g roasted, salted peanuts
150g sunflower oil
75g dried crispy shallots or onions
5 garlic cloves, thinly sliced
1 tbsp coriander seeds
5cm orange peel, white pith removed
1 tbsp sesame seeds (optional)
1 tbsp sugar
1 tsp fine sea salt

Add the chillies and peanuts to the bowl of a food processor and blitz until the peanuts are a rubble and the chilli is small-to-medium flaked, about 10 to 12 pulses. Warm the oil in a saucepan over a medium heat, add the fried shallots or onions and fry for about 2 minutes. Add the chilli and peanuts, reduce the heat so the mixture slowly bubbles for 2 to 3 minutes, then add the garlic, coriander seeds, orange peel, sesame seeds, if using, sugar and salt. Simmer for 5 minutes, then remove from the heat and allow to cool completely before transferring to a clean container or jar.

Tahini Dressing

Drizzle over falafels or a salad.

2 tbsp tahini
2 tbsp lemon juice
1 garlic clove, grated
sea salt

In a small bowl whisk together the tahini, lemon juice and 2 tablespoons of warm water. Add a grated garlic clove, season with salt and whisk again until smooth.

Zhoug

An emerald green, spicy, fragrant sauce to serve with falafels, tortilla, chargrilled steak and grilled chicken. Makes enough for a main dish for four but any extra will keep well in a jar in the fridge.

50g fresh coriander, leaves and stems roughly chopped
25g fresh flat-leaf parsley, larger stems removed, leaves chopped
2–3 plump green chillies, de-seeded and chopped
3 garlic cloves, peeled and finely chopped
1 tsp ground cumin
1 tsp ground coriander
1 tsp coriander seeds
1 tsp ground cardamom
juice of 1 lemon
½ tsp sea salt
75ml olive oil

In a food processor or in a jug with a stick blender, combine all the ingredients except for the olive oil and blitz until it all starts to come together. Add the olive oil in a fine stream as you blitz and a sauce will form. Taste and use straight away or store for up to a week in a clean jar in the fridge.

Walnut Salsa

A fresh and tangy salsa that's as delicious with the aubergine pasta on p.107 as it is with cheese and crackers.

150g walnuts
zest and juice of ½ lemon
1 tsp chopped fresh rosemary
2 tbsp olive oil
1 tbsp sherry vinegar or red wine vinegar
fine sea salt and freshly ground black pepper

Preheat the oven to 200°C/180°C fan. Line a baking tray with greaseproof paper, arrange the walnuts on it and bake for 8 minutes or until golden. When cool, break the nuts up with your hands, add to a bowl and mix with the lemon zest and juice, rosemary, olive oil, vinegar and seasoning.

Wonderful Fries

Seriously moreish, roasted, golden new potatoes.

Serves 4

500g small new potatoes, as evenly sized as possible
4 tbsp (60ml) olive oil
1 tsp garlic powder
150g crème fraîche or soured cream
10g flat-leaf parsley, finely chopped
sea salt

Put the potatoes in a large pan, add cold water to cover and a tablespoon of salt. Bring to a boil over a medium heat, then turn down and simmer until the potatoes are tender but not falling apart, 15 to 18 minutes. Drain well.

Meanwhile preheat the oven to 200°C/180°C fan. Line a rimmed baking tray with greaseproof paper, drizzle over a tablespoon of the olive oil and sprinkle lightly with salt. Tip the cooked potatoes onto the prepared baking tray and, using a chopping board, press down on them to gently but evenly crush them. Sprinkle over the garlic powder, drizzle with the remaining 3 tablespoons of olive oil and season with a big pinch of salt. Roast in the oven for 30 minutes, or until deeply golden with crispy edges. Serve hot with dollops of crème fraîche or soured cream and a scattering of the chopped flat-leaf parsley.

Flatbreads

Add chopped chives or wild garlic, dried oregano or ras el hanout to the dough for extra flavour. For a wholewheat version, substitute half of the self-raising flour with wholewheat flour. These freeze well – just reheat for 10 minutes at 180°C/160°C fan.

Makes 10–12

500g self-raising flour plus a little extra for rolling
1 tbsp baking powder
10g fine sea salt
500g natural yoghurt
1–2 tbsp olive oil for frying

You can make the dough by hand or with a food processor. If by hand: in a large mixing bowl, whisk together the self-raising flour, baking powder and salt. Add the yoghurt to the dry ingredients and mix with a spatula until a dough starts to form. If by food processor: add the self-raising flour, baking powder, salt and yoghurt to the bowl of the food processor. Pulse in 2-second bursts about ten times until the mix forms a ball.

Tip the dough out onto a lightly floured surface and knead for a minute, until smooth. Divide the dough into equally sized small balls and, on a lightly floured surface, roll each into a round flatbread shape about 5mm thick.

Heat a non-stick skillet or griddle over medium heat and brush it with olive oil. Cook the flatbreads for 2 to 3 minutes on each side, until golden brown and slightly puffed. Remove from the skillet and keep warm under clean tea towels until ready to serve.

Focaccia

Feel free to add any topping you like to this basic recipe. Try olives, caramelised onions, roasted red peppers, rosemary, cheese, fresh figs or sliced nectarines. You can mix the dough and leave it to rise for as little as 2 hours, or you can prepare it in advance and leave it in the fridge for up to 36 hours.

Serves 6–8

1 × 7g sachet instant yeast
1/4 tsp sugar
450ml warm water
500g bread flour
10g sea salt
2 tbsp olive oil
Maldon salt for sprinkling on top

high-sided baking tin approx. 33cm x 23cm lined with greaseproof and a drizzle of olive oil

Mix the yeast, sugar and 50ml of the warm water in a cup and set aside until frothy, about 5 minutes.

In a large mixing bowl, combine the flour, salt, remaining 400ml of warm water and the yeast mixture. Using a spatula, stir until everything is completely combined and you have a sticky dough. Make sure to incorporate the flour on the sides of the bowl. Drizzle a tablespoon of olive oil over the dough in the bowl and use your fingertips to spread it over the top to stop it drying out. Leave the dough in the bowl in a warm place for 1 1/2 to 2 hours, until it has doubled in size.

If preparing the dough in advance, wrap the bowl in cling film or put a lid on it and put it in the fridge for at least 8 hours and up to 36 hours.

When you're ready, tip the dough into your prepared baking tin, using a spatula to scrape any clingy dough from the bowl. Push the dough towards the edges and the corners of the tin, sprinkle over the second tablespoon of olive oil and use your fingertips to dimple the top of the dough. Rest the dough in a warm place for half an hour. It will rise again and bubbles will start to form on the top.

Preheat the oven to 220°C/200°C fan while the dough is resting. Sprinkle with salt, or the toppings of your choice, and bake for 30 minutes or until golden and springy to the touch.

A

asparagus
    Ruffled Filo Asparagus Tart 42
    Spring Risotto with Asparagus and Lime 52
aubergine
    Spicy Aubergine Rigatoni 107

B

Barley Risotto with Cider and Bacon 135
beans
    Hearty Tuscan Bean Stew 104
    White Bean and Winter Veg Stew 10
beef
    Brisket 124
    Rosemary-Lemon Flat Iron Steak and Oven Chips 78
    Soy Mirin Steak Noodles 17
beetroot
    Neon Pasta 72
Brisket 124
Bruschetta with Summer Tomatoes, Burrata and Basil 85
Brussels sprouts
    St Clements Brussels Sprouts with Garlicky Puy Lentils 128
Bubble and Squeak 24
butternut squash
    Spiced Butternut Pilaf 97

C

Cacio e Pepe 22
cauliflower
    Roasted Cauliflower Tacos (variation) 67
Cauliflower Croque Monsieur 116
Caramelised Onion Galette with Manchego, Fresh Figs and Thyme 94
Cheddar and Parsley Spanish Tortilla 62
chicken
    Coq au Vin 121
    Dijon Honey Chicken Thighs 27
    Lemon Roast Spatchcock Chicken 132
    Pretzel Chicken with Apple Slaw 110
    Shawarma with Lemon and Garlic Potatoes 88
    Sticky Lemongrass Chicken Salad 68
    Tarragon and Crème Fraîche Chicken 100
Chicken Cacciatore 14
Chilli Crisp 136
Citrus Chicken Couscous 77
Coq au Vin 121
Creamy Cheese Tortellini 21
Crispy Coconut Prawns and Pineapple Salsa 86
Crofter's Pie 123

D

dhal
    Sri Lankan-style Dhal 31
Dijon Honey Chicken Thighs 27

E

eggs
    Cheddar and Parsley Spanish Tortilla 62

F

falafel
    Quick and Easy Falafels 55
filo
    Ruffled Asparagus Filo Tart
fish
    Kedgeree 109
    Roasted Salmon Tacos with Avocado Crema 66
    Salmon en Croute with Lemon Thyme 131
    Sea Bass with Lime, Courgette and Ginger 74
    Trout with Herb and Lime Crust 57
Fish Pie 98
Flatbreads 138
Focaccia 139

G

galette
    Caramelised Onion Galette with Manchego, Fresh Figs and Thyme 94

gnudi
    Wild Garlic Gnudi with Brown Butter and
    Lemon

H

haggis
    Crofters Pie 123
Hearty Tuscan Bean Stew 104
Herby Rice and Citrus Prawns 34

I

Infallible Sesame Noodles with Peanut
    Sauce 82

K

Kedgeree 109
kofta
    Lamb Koftas with Green Sauce 90

L

laksa
    Delicious Vegan Laksa 46
Lamb Koftas with Green Sauce 90
Lemon Roast Spatchcock Chicken 132
lentils
    Sri Lankan-style Dhal 31
    St Clements Brussels Sprouts with
    Garlicky Puy Lentils 128

M

meatballs
    Turkey Meatballs with Tahini Sauce 48
mushroom
    Mushroom Risotto (variation) 52
    Shawarma with Lemon and Garlic
    Potatoes 88
Mussels with White Wine, Crème Fraîche
    and Parsley 119

N

Neon Pasta 72

noodles
    Delicious Vegan Laksa 46
    Infallible Sesame Noodles with Peanut
    Sauce 82
    Soy Mirin Steak Noodles 17

P

pasta
    Cacio e Pepe 22
    Creamy Cheese Tortellini 21
    Neon Pasta 72
    Rigatoni Marinara with Bacon and
    Rosemary Breadcrumbs 58
    Spaghetti Aglio e Olio 65
    Spicy Aubergine Rigatoni 107
peanut
    Infallible Sesame Noodles with Peanut
    Sauce 82
pie
    Crofter's Pie 123
potatoes
    Bubble and Squeak 24
    Rosemary-Lemon Flat Iron Steak and
    Oven Chips 78
    Wonderful Fries 138
prawns
    Crispy Coconut Prawns and Pineapple
    Salsa 86
    Herby Rice and Citrus Prawns 34
    Pretzel Chicken with Apple Slaw 110

Q

Quick and Easy Falafels 55

R

Red Onion Gravy 36
rice
    Herby Rice and Citrus Prawns 34
    Spiced Butternut Pilaf 97
    Spring Risotto with Asparagus and Lime
    52
    Stir Fried Rice 12
rice paper

Vietnamese Rice Paper Rolls 45
Rigatoni Marinara with Bacon and
  Rosemary Breadcrumbs 58
risotto
  Spring Risotto with Asparagus and Lime
  52
Roast Gnocchi with Sausages, Apples and
  Shallots 113
Roasted Cauliflower Tacos (variation) 67
Roasted Salmon Tacos with Avocado
  Crema 66
Rosemary-Lemon Flat Iron Steak and Oven
  Chips 78
Ruffled Filo Asparagus Tart 42

S

salad
  Sticky Lemongrass Chicken Salad 68
salmon
  Roasted Salmon Tacos with Avocado
  Crema 66
Salmon en Croute with Lemon Thyme 131
sausages
  Roast Gnocchi with Sausages, Apples
  and Shallots 113
  Toad in the Hole with Red Onion Gravy
  36
Sea Bass with Lime, Courgette and
  Ginger 74
Shawarma with Lemon and Garlic
  Potatoes 88
Soy Mirin Steak Noodles 17
Spaghetti Aglio e Olio 65
Spiced Butternut Pilaf 97
Spicy Aubergine Rigatoni 107
Spring Risotto with Asparagus and Lime 52
Sri Lankan-style Dhal 31
St Clements Brussels Sprouts with Garlicky
  Puy Lentils 128
steak
  Rosemary-Lemon Flat Iron Steak and
  Oven Chips 78
  Soy Mirin Steak Noodles 17
Sticky Lemongrass Chicken Salad 68
Stir Fried Rice 12

T

tacos
  Roasted Cauliflower Tacos (variation) 67
  Roasted Salmon Tacos with Avocado
  Crema 66
Tahini Dressing 136
Tarragon and Crème Fraîche Chicken 100
tart
  Ruffled Filo Asparagus Tart 42
Tempura Everything 33
Toad in the Hole with Red Onion Gravy 36
tomatoes
  Bruschetta with Summer Tomatoes,
  Burrata and Basil 85
tortellini
  Creamy Cheese Tortellini 21
tortilla
  Cheddar and Parsley Spanish Tortilla 62
Trout with Herb and Lime Crust 57
Turkey Meatballs with Tahini Sauce 48

V

Vegan Laksa 46
Vietnamese Rice Paper Rolls 45

W

Walnut Salsa 137
White Bean and Winter Veg Stew 10
Wild Garlic Gnudi with Brown Butter and
  Lemon 41
Wonderful Fries 138

Z

Zhoug 137

pea shoots

Acknowledgements

Thanks and huge love to Nasim Doherty and Emily Dewhurst, who guided, styled and edited so generously, to Bethany Ferguson who styled the food so expertly and to Claire Irwin, who shot it all so beautifully.

Thanks for recipe testing and invaluable creative input to Helen, Mark, Magnus and Ben Hampton; Cat, Tony, Heather and Laura; the legendary Sam Gardener, the inspirational Nicola Cooper and the mighty strong Victoria and Ruby.

Thanks to Look Out Skateboards; Nicky and Ali; Andy, Seb, Amy and the Heart Buchanan OGs and Scott at Lab Espresso; Max the Pirate, Emili, Paul, Gillian and Rachel; David and Scott; and the incredible Rachel Meddowes and the Smart Works team.

And thanks most of all to my mum, for her wisdom and patience, and to my son Lucas, for his forebearance whilst we tested recipes. He is my light.

Kitchen Press would like to thank Thea Bryant for the illustrations of seasonal fruit and vegetables and ceramicist Geoff Calder of Stockbridge Ceramics in Edinburgh (stockbridgeceramics.com) for the loan of many of the beautiful hand-thrown bowls and plates that appear throughout this book.